Learn and Play in the Garden

C. 1
1999
18.95

All inquiries should be addressed to:
Barron's Educational Series, Inc.
250 Wireless Boulevard
Hauppauge, New York 11788

Library of Congress Catalog Card No. 96-86075

ISBN 0-8120-9780-7

PRINTED IN HONG KONG
98765432

Learn and Play in the Garden

Meg Herd

FOREST HOUSE ®

School & Library Edition

C O N T

tomat

Beans

...ENTS

Autumn

Winter

Glossary

Parents Guide

A garden is a wonderfully interesting and exciting place in which children can play, work, and learn.

This book encourages children of all ages, from toddlers to young teenagers, to take full advantage of garden space. The book is organized by season, including seasonal activities through which children are introduced to gardening tasks, recipes using homegrown produce, natural science experiments, imaginative play, craft activities using nature's bounty, and run and fun games that are ideally played out in the fresh air. Emphasis is on learning through fun.

Ages and Stages

Children of all ages are interested in and can develop through activities in the garden.

Those as young as two years old enjoy toddling around the garden, picking flowers, watering, or digging with a toy spade. Touch, smell, and taste are important for cognitive development at this age, so parents need to be aware of the dangers of eating some plants and to be vigilant with supervision. Gross-motor and fine-motor skills, language development, and coordination can all be fostered in two- to four-year-olds with garden-based activities.

From four years on, children are eager to undertake more focused gardening tasks. Planting seeds and watching them grow is an absorbing pastime for this age group. It is an ideal age to make a first vegetable garden. Cooking will flow naturally from children raising their own produce—they will be eager to pick and prepare the fruits of their labor.

The beginning stages of children's ability to distinguish and name basic plant parts—leaves, petals, flowers, stems, and roots—will emerge between the ages of four and six. It is timely to introduce a simple explanation of the function of these plant parts.

Pruning is enjoyed by four- to eight-year-olds. Given a small pair of safety scissors, enthusiastic young gardeners can quite safely deadhead (cut off the older flowers) their annuals, trim the grass around bed edges, or pick flowers for their own rooms.

From age eight onward, the garden and its creatures will provide a rich resource for scientific observation and experimentation. You can introduce botanical concepts to children and encourage an interest in all flora and fauna. Growth patterns, life cycles, propagation, pollination, photosynthesis, insect and bird behavior, and climatic changes can be observed and studied in the garden, at close range and in a meaningful context.

Older children will want to observe some of the garden's more novel phenomena. Plant growth movements (tropisms), short- and long-day plants (photoperiodism), growing giant or baby cultivars, and plant reproduction will attract their attention.

Getting Started

TOOLS OF THE TRADE

- pots and containers
- potting mix (see Spring, Good-quality Potting Mix, p. 25) for propagating seeds, available at nurseries
- seeds
- seedlings

- bulbs
- fertilizer
- a trowel
- growing space in the garden
- a watering can

Children living in an apartment need not miss out on the joy of gardening. Pots or containers on balconies can be filled with annuals or some of the smaller growing vegetables. Strawberries raised in pots are a delight for children to grow and eat. Bulbs flourish in containers and will grow indoors. A sunny windowsill is ideal for herbs in pots. There are also many indoor gardening activities listed in this book that will arouse a child's interest in propagating, growing, and nurturing plants.

Handy Hints

- Don't relegate a child's growing garden area to the worst part of the garden. To be successful gardeners, children need a good site: sunny with good soil.
- Direct without doing: guide and advise without doing the job for them. Children are capable of digging, selecting plants, sowing seed or planting seedlings, fertilizing, watering, and harvesting. Be enthusiastic! Children will follow your lead.
- Use a hands-on approach: children are best equipped to come to an understanding of a concept if they actively use all their senses to explore an object or concept. Gardening is an ultimate hands-on experience for children. By touching, smelling, listening, watching, and tasting, the child will develop an intimate knowledge of and an empathy for plants and nature.
- Children can have relatively short attention spans and may need quick results to maintain their interest in an activity; for this reason, quick-growing plants like salad greens, vegetables, and annuals are ideal first gardening projects.

Seed Supplies

This book offers children ideas for a number of seed-raising projects. Most of the seeds can be collected from the garden or kitchen. Save vegetable seeds—pumpkin, winter squash, peas, sweet pepper, tomato, avocado—to propagate at a later stage. Fruit pips and seeds from apple, passion fruit, mango, orange, lemon, or any of the stone fruits also work well. Other seeds are readily available at the local plant nursery or garden section of the supermarket. There are a few unusual cultivars listed that may need to be searched out. Try contacting specialist seed companies, seed-saving networks, and heritage or rare seed suppliers. Listings for specialist seed suppliers can be found in the yellow pages and in the back pages of gardening magazines. These companies are happy to supply catalogs (usually free of charge) through mail order.

Safety First

With parental supervision and guidance, the garden is a place where children can be free to run, climb, and explore, and to dig in the soil and get their hands dirty. It is a place where they can learn and play while toiling over their crops, observing the garden's creatures, and actively experimenting with plants and seeds and growing things.

However, it is not always a harmless place. Safety in the garden is of paramount importance. Here are some dangers to watch out for.

- Many gardening tools are sharp, such as pruning shears, forks, and rakes. Don't allow children to use any sharp tool unsupervised. Keep such implements out of reach.
- Children will invariably get small cuts and scratches while gardening, despite careful supervision. Clean any cuts with disinfectant immediately. Make sure your children's tetanus injections are up to date.
- Do not allow children to use pesticides, fungicides, insecticides, or herbicides. Keep them in a locked, child-proof cabinet.
- Keep the phone number of your local doctor and the Poison Control Center in a handy place to ensure swift action if a poisoning does occur.
- Not all garden creatures are harmless. Spiders live in gardens and a few are dangerous. If a child is bitten, contact your doctor or Poison Control Center.
- Some plants are toxic. Contact your doctor or Poison Control Center if your child displays symptoms of poisoning.
- Supervise any activity involving water. Children can drown in a very small amount of water.
- Supervise and help with craft and cooking activities that may require the use of a knife or require other difficult tasks.
- When paint is required for craft activities, be sure to use nontoxic paint.

COMMON AND BOTANICAL NAMES LIST

Usually, common names have been used in this book. Because common names can differ from one country to another, and because different plants can have the same common name, reference may have to be made to the botanical name.

COMMON NAME	BOTANICAL NAME
Autumn crocus	Zephranthes candida
Belladonna lily	Amaryllis belladonna
Bluebell	Endymion spp.
Catmint	Nepeta mussinii
Catnip	Nepeta cataria
Cinnamon tree	Cinnamomum camphora
Cork oak	Quercus suber
Cuban lily	Scilla peruviana
Daffodil	Narcissus spp.
English daisy	Bellis perennis
Fairy primrose	Primula malacoides
Freesia	Freesia x hybrida
Grape hyacinth	Muscari botryoides
Amaryllis	Hippeastrum
Hyacinth	Hyacinthus orientalis
Jacobean lily	Sprekelia formosissima
Jonquil	Narcissus spp.
Lily of the valley	Convallaria majalis
Nasturtium	Tropaeolum majus
Nerine	Nerine bowdenii
Strawflower	Helichrysum bracteatum
Passion fruit	Passiflora edulis
Polyanthus	Primula x polyantha
Pot marigold	Calendula officinalis
Ranunculus	Ranunculus asiaticus
Scarborough lily	Vallota speciosa
Scarlet sage	Salvia splendens
Snowdrop	Galanthus nivalis
Snowflake	Leucojum vernum
Spring star-flower	Ipheion uniflorum
Statice	Limonium latifolium
Sweet pea	Lathyrus odoratus
Tulip	Tulipa spp.

S P R

Garden Discovery in Spring

In springtime, gardens are bursting with life: trees and shrubs are budding with the promise of abundant flowers to come. This season is the beginning of the cycle of life for both plants and animals, and a good time to be exploring the garden for signs of new life.

It is also the best time to do lots of groundwork: get the soil ready for a vegetable bed or a strawberry patch. Growing and cooking can go hand in hand when you harvest your own produce! Try vegetable soup or strawberry jam.

Insects are at their peak: look for beetles, bugs, and butterflies.

•••

Prepare soil and plant seeds in spring so you can harvest lots of healthy, fresh vegetables.

•••

Creating Your Own Vegetable Garden

Making your own vegetable garden and growing some favorite vegetables will be an exciting gardening task. If you tend your crops carefully, you will be able to harvest fresh, healthy food for yourself and your family.

You will need some adult help to begin with, in order to find a space and dig the garden. After that, choose the vegetables you want to grow, save up and buy your own seeds or seedlings, and plant them. You must remember to water and fertilize regularly and check your plants for pests. When your plants mature, you will be rewarded for your efforts by a basketful of healthy produce that is fresh, tasty, and nutritious.

It is a good idea to get all your ideas on paper first—make lists of vegetables you want to grow and where you will plant them.

❖❖❖

How to Make a Vegetable Garden

1. DRAW UP A PLAN

Draw an outline of your garden on a large sheet of paper or cardboard and mark in where you are going to place each type of vegetable. Refer to your plan when planting.

2. CHOOSE A SITE

Choose a sunny position, away from large trees. The spot should be level, protected from gusty winds and close to a water faucet or hose connection.

3. GET THE GARDEN PLOT READY

With an adult helper, mark the outline of your plot or bed with a piece of rope or a hose. If the area is lawn covered, remove the grass. Dig over the top of the soil to a depth of 8 inches (20 cm).

Add animal manure, compost (for a method to make compost, see Winter, A Worm Farm, p. 122) or complete fertilizer and allow the soil to rest for several weeks. Pull out any weeds that begin to grow.

Just before planting, dig the bed again to break down the soil into small, crumbly particles. Rake the bed so the soil is even. This will make a fine seedbed for your vegetables.

Dig over the topsoil until it is even and crumbly so when you plant your seeds, they will have a good chance of growing well.

4. SELECT AND PLANT YOUR VEGETABLE SEEDLINGS

Supermarkets and garden centers have stands displaying all types of vegetable seeds and seedlings. Have a good look and decide which varieties you would like to grow.

On the back of the seed packet, you will find information about the best time to plant, how deep to place the seeds, how far apart to space seeds, as well as how to look after your plants.

5. LABEL YOUR PLANTS

It is sometimes hard to remember what you have planted where, especially when using seed, so it is a good idea to label your vegetable bed as you are planting.

GARDENING TIP

🌳 🌳 🌳 🌳

SEEDS OR SEEDLINGS?

To begin growing vegetables you can use either seeds from a packet or seedlings grown in a pot of soil. Seedlings are small plants that have grown from seeds to about 2 inches (5 cm) high. Growing vegetables from seed is cheaper, but using seedlings means you will be able to harvest quicker as the plant has already been growing for 2–3 weeks in a pot. Some vegetables do not like being transplanted and grow better when planted directly into their permanent position in the plot. Examples are carrots, radishes, and beets.

Planting seedlings in neat rows means there is no wasted space in your vegetable plot.

◆◆◆

Vegetable Labels

YOU WILL NEED

- stiff plastic, cut into rectangles
- pictures of vegetables from magazines or from the front of seed packets
- safety scissors
- Popsicle sticks
- craft glue

WHAT TO DO

Cut out pictures of the vegetables you are planting.

Glue the pictures onto the plastic rectangles.

Put a little glue on the top end of the required number of Popsicle sticks.

Press the sticks onto the backs of the plastic rectangles. Allow to dry, then place each stick in front of the row of vegetables it represents.

6. LOOK AFTER YOUR PLANTS

Vegetables love water. Go out to your garden area regularly to see if your plants are wilting or if the ground is dry. Give them a drink if they need it.

Fertilize regularly by scattering a complete fertilizer around the ground close to the plants. This is called broadcasting. You could also use a fertilizer that dissolves in water. Look on the back of the package and it will tell you the correct amount of fertilizer and water to use. Spoon the fertilizer into a watering can, add the proper amount of water, and stir until the fertilizer is dissolved. Pour it around the roots and over the leaves of your plants.

Scatter fertilizer around your vegetables and they will soon grow into strong plants.

♦♦♦

Capsicum

Beans

Carrot

beetroot

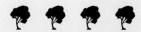

GARDENING TIP

🌳 🌳 🌳 🌳

WATERING PLANTS

- Don't water your plants every day. First, look at them to see if they are wilting, or feel down in the soil to see if it is dry.
- Water early in the morning or late in the afternoon when the temperature is cooler, so that less water is lost in evaporation.
- When hosing, stand about 3 feet (1 m) away from the plants.
- Don't have the water pressure too high or the plants may be damaged, and the soil disturbed, by the jet.
- Only water the area around the plants: not the fences or walls by swinging the hose around. Water the ground around the plants rather than the leaves.
- Give your plants a thorough soaking when they need it rather than little drinks now and again.
- Water your potted plants with a small watering can. Feel whether the potting mix is dry before watering. When dry, give your plant a good soaking, until water drips out of the hole in the bottom of the pot.
- Water vegetables and annuals more often than other plants. This is necessary because they have a small root system supplying moisture to a large leaf area.

Safe Spraying

Sometimes you will have to spray to get rid of pests in the garden, especially if you are growing your own vegetables or have a prized annual plot. You can make and use safe organic sprays that will not be harmful to you, your family, or all the good insects in the area.

Garlic Spray

YOU WILL NEED

- several cloves of garlic
- 32 fluid ounces (1 l) water
- a large bottle or bucket
- a spray bottle

WHAT TO DO

Crush the cloves of garlic.
Soak in the water overnight.
Remove the pieces of garlic in the morning.
Pour the liquid into your sprayer.
Spray over leaves to stop caterpillars and other leaf-eating or sucking insects from munching your plants.

Soap Spray

YOU WILL NEED

- soap scraps (make sure you use soap and not detergent for this recipe)
- a jar
- 32 fluid ounces (1 l) cold water
- warm water
- a spray bottle

WHAT TO DO

Place some scraps of soap in a jar.
Add warm water to cover the soap.
Soak until the soap softens and turns to jelly.
Mix a tablespoon of the jelly in the cold water and stir well.
Pour into your sprayer and use for aphids and other pest bugs.
Spray plants well in areas where aphids are living. The soapy water must cover the aphids to be effective.

♦ *Use safe sprays when getting rid of insect pests on your plants.* ♦

What to Grow

Choose vegetables that you enjoy eating and that are easy to grow. Snow peas, beans, lettuce, radish, pumpkin, zucchini, Swiss chard, carrots, tomato, Chinese cabbage, sweet pepper, and green shallots (spring onions) will not give you any trouble. Fast-growing, leafy salad greens such as Romaine lettuce as well as Chinese cabbage would be good beginners' choices.

Four Easy-to-grow Vegetables Step by Step

ZUCCHINI

Select a zucchini variety that suits your needs. Most zucchini plants are space hogs as they have huge leaves and grow on long spreading vines. If you don't have a large area, choose a bush type, such as Gold Rush: it will grow into a compact bush and produce a lot of fruit with a golden yellow skin. It is even small enough to grow in a large container.

Sow the seed any time in spring, at a depth of ½ inch (1.3 cm).

Space seeds 3 feet (1 m) apart, if you are planting more than one seed.

Feed and water regularly. Zucchini love water and fertilizer.

Harvest in 7–8 weeks when the zucchini are ripe.

DID YOU KNOW?

When you eat vegetables, you are eating the leaves, fruit, flowers, stems, seeds, or roots of a plant. To see what part you are eating look at the chart below!

FLOWERS	broccoli, cauliflower
FLOWER BUDS	brussels sprouts
FRUIT	tomatoes, melons, zucchini, marrows, squash, chayotes, sweet peppers, pumpkins, cucumbers, eggplants
LEAVES	lettuce, spinach, cabbage, Swiss chard
PODS AND SEEDS	sweet corn, peas, beans, snow peas
ROOTS	carrots, parsnips, radishes, beets
ROOT TUBER	potatoes
STEMS	rhubarb, celery, asparagus
BULBS (swollen stems)	chives, onions, leeks, green shallots (spring onions), garlic

•••

Planting beans is easy because the seeds are large. If you choose a climbing variety, you will need a support for them like this tripod.

•••

GARDENING TIP

COMPANION PLANTING

Some plants are so happy growing next to each other that their health and development improve and they will give you better yields. On the other hand, some plants hate living close together and will stunt each other's growth.

Experiment with some of the following plant combinations to see if planting companions or friends close together makes a difference.

• Tomatoes grow well when planted with basil or parsley.

• Tomatoes and carrots grow well together, but tomatoes and broccoli do not get on at all.

• Lettuce likes to be with carrots, radishes, and cucumbers.

• Beans and peas do not do well when near onions and garlic.

• Sweet corn is a good neighbor for pumpkins.

• Zucchini thrive next to beans or radishes.

• Potatoes and pumpkins are not happy together.

18

BEANS

Select a dwarf or bush bean variety such as "Tendercrop," that only grows to 20 inches (51 cm), so you will not need to stake the plants. (Most bean plants are climbers and can grow to about 6 feet (2 m) or more and have to be tied up on a stake.)

Sow the seed in warm soil in early spring.

Make a shallow furrow (or a small trench) 1½–2 inches (4–5 cm) deep.

Place each seed 4 inches (10 cm) apart, along the furrow.

Cover lightly with soil and press down firmly.

Water gently.

Wait until your seeds start sprouting and then feed every 2 weeks with a liquid fertilizer. Bean seeds do not like direct contact with fertilizer at the planting stage.

Pick your first beans in 8–10 weeks. They are crunchy and delicious when eaten right after harvesting! Remember, the more you pick the more you get, because the plant's energy is moved from maturing the fruit to making more flowers that will develop into more beans.

CARROTS

Sow carrot seed at any time of the year, except for winter. The seed is quite small. Mixing it with some dry sand first makes it easier to sprinkle evenly over the bed.

Plant the seeds directly in the spot you want to grow them: carrots don't like being transplanted. Choose a sunny position.

Cover the seeds lightly with soil.

Water your carrots regularly. If the soil goes from wet to dry all the time, the carrot roots will crack and split.

Fertilize only after the carrots begin growing so the roots will be well shaped. Carrots, like all the other root crops, may grow into funny shapes if the soil has had fresh animal manure added to it at planting time.

Pull your carrots in 4–5 months when they are fully grown.

Note: The orange color of carrots depends on the variety and temperature. Between 61°F (16°C) and 70°F (21°C) the roots will develop a deep orange color. If cooler or hotter than this, they will probably be paler in color.

RADISHES

Choose radishes if you are growing vegetables for the first time. They are quick to grow and do not need much care.

Sow the seeds at any time of the year, except during winter in cold climates.

Cover lightly with a sandy soil mixture.

Water gently. Within a week, seeds will have germinated and the leaves of the seedlings will be showing. Be sure to water regularly.

Apply liquid fertilizer every 2 weeks to keep them growing quickly. Slow growth makes radishes taste bitter.

Pull the radishes in 4–6 weeks when they are ready to eat.

Cooking Your Vegetables

Make your own vegetable garden and you will be able to harvest fresh, healthy produce. You can use your vegetables to make delicious preserves, cakes, desserts, pies, or soups. Try making vegetable soup with any combination of your favorite vegetables.

Tomato sauce is easy to make and very nutritious. You could bake a carrot cake for a delicious school lunch treat. With adult help for using the microwave, blending, and cutting you can enjoy the process of cooking crops you have raised.

Vegetable Soup

YOU WILL NEED

- some of the vegetables growing in your garden, which may include:
    carrots, potatoes, tomatoes, cauliflower, beans, broccoli, peas, onion, zucchini, sweet corn, sweet peppers, celery
- a wooden board
- a sharp knife
- a large microwave-safe casserole dish
- a wooden spoon
- boiling water and a bouillon cube (chicken, beef or vegetable)
- if you have a herb plot or herbs growing in containers, pick a handful of parsley and chives to add to your soup (or buy some from the supermarket).

WHAT TO DO

Wash, peel, and chop the vegetables into bite-sized pieces. Ask an adult to do the chopping.
Place ingredients into the casserole dish and just cover with the water or bouillon.
Cover with the lid.
Cook in the microwave on HIGH (100% power) for about 15 minutes or until the vegetables are tender. Ask an adult to help with the microwave.

Stir the soup once or twice during cooking.
Chop the parsley and chives (ask an adult to help you chop the herbs).
Stir the chopped parsley and chives into the soup just before serving.

Tomato Sauce

YOU WILL NEED

- 6 large tomatoes, peeled and chopped (see Cooking Tip)
- 1 small carrot, peeled and grated
- 1 small apple, peeled, cored, and chopped
- 1 small onion, peeled and chopped
- ¼ teaspoon salt
- 1 tablespoon sugar
- 1 chicken bouillon cube
- 1 tablespoon tomato paste
- a wooden board
- a vegetable peeler
- a sharp knife
- a grater
- a large microwave-safe casserole dish
- a wooden spoon
- an electric blender
- a ladle
- a rubber spatula
- a clean jar or bottle

♦ Shelling peas for vegetable soup is fun. ♦

WHAT TO DO

Place all the ingredients in the casserole dish, and cover.

Cook in the microwave on HIGH (100% power) for about 12 minutes or until the vegetables are well cooked; stir once or twice during cooking.

Spoon the mixture into the blender jug; cover and blend until completely smooth.

Pour into the jar or bottle, scraping all the sauce out of the jug with the spatula.

Note: This sauce will keep for a few days in the refrigerator or can be frozen for up to 2 months.

COOKING TIP

HOW TO PEEL TOMATOES

Tomatoes need to be peeled before they are cooked and made into sauce, however fresh tomatoes are difficult to peel. To make the job easier, first remove the core and cut a cross in the skin. Next, place the tomatoes in a bowl and cook in the microwave for 3 minutes on HIGH (100% power). Cool a little. The skin will peel off without trouble.

Carrot Cake

YOU WILL NEED

- ½ cup (125 ml) oil
- ¾ cup (150 g) brown sugar
- 3 eggs
- 1 teaspoon vanilla extract
- 2 cups finely grated carrot (about 3–4 large carrots)
- 1 cup canned crushed pineapple, including juice
- 2 cups (300 g) self-rising flour
- 1 teaspoon ground nutmeg
- ½ teaspoon ground cinnamon
- a large mixing bowl
- a wooden spoon
- a grater
- a sifter
- an 8-inch (20 cm) microwave-safe tube pan
- a wire rack

WHAT TO DO

Mix the oil and sugar in a large bowl, stirring well with the wooden spoon.

Beat in the eggs, one at a time, beating well between additions.

Add the vanilla extract, carrot, and pineapple.

Sift the flour and spices together, then add them to the bowl and mix well.

Oil the cake pan and pour the cake mixture into it, scraping all the mixture out of the bowl.

Cook in the microwave oven on HIGH (100% power) for 10 minutes, then let sit in the microwave for 5 minutes.

Remove the pan from the microwave and turn the cake onto a wire rack to cool.

Ice the cooled cake evenly with lemon cream cheese icing.

Lemon Cream Cheese Icing

YOU WILL NEED

- 1½ cups (240 g) powdered sugar
- 2 ounces (60 g) cream cheese, softened
- 1 ounce (30 g) butter, softened
- 2 teaspoons fresh lemon juice
- a sifter
- a hand electric mixer
- a large mixing bowl
- a rubber spatula

WHAT TO DO

Sift the powdered sugar into the mixing bowl.

Add the cream cheese and butter. Beat on low speed, using the mixer, until all the ingredients are combined.

Add the lemon juice.

Beat on high speed until the sugar is light and fluffy, occasionally scraping down the sides of the bowl with the rubber spatula.

Sally Scarecrow

You might find that birds in your neighborhood enjoy eating your vegetables as much as you do and they will swoop down to gobble up the choicest morsels.

To stop all your produce from being devoured, try making a scarecrow to guard your patch. Sally Scarecrow is made from a mop, a pumpkin face, and old clothes filled with straw.

You can use any materials for your scarecrow. Old brooms and mops are handy for arms or legs or to keep the head and body together. Straw or scrunched-up newspaper is useful for stuffing the body. Save your old clothes to dress it up.

You will have to use a strong, heavy pole to support a big scarecrow like Sally. Ask an adult to help you find a metal stake on which to tie the scarecrow and to help you erect it securely in your vegetable garden.

Sally Scarecrow will scare off even the bravest of birds from your vegetable crops and watch over your garden.
◆ ◆ ◆

CRAFT TIP

You can make a quick and easy scarecrow, by cutting a body shape from stiff cardboard. Glue pieces of fabric on for clothes and wool for hair. Draw the scarecrow's eyes, nose, and mouth directly on the cardboard. Tie your scarecrow onto a broom handle and place it in your vegetable plot.

Succulent Strawberries

Strawberries are an easy crop to grow and are much tastier than store-bought ones. They don't take up much space in the garden. You can even grow them in pots. Although they fruit mainly in summer, you might be lucky enough to pick a strawberry or two throughout the year.

•••

Strawberry plants send out long stems called runners. A new baby plant grows on the end of the runner, where it touches the ground. Cut off the baby plant, put it in a pot or plant it in your strawberry patch. It will grow and produce more strawberries.

•••

How to Grow Strawberries

YOU WILL NEED

- small potted strawberry plants (buy from a nursery or collect runners from a friend who has strawberry plants growing)
- a sunny plot in the garden with well-drained soil
- compost
- fertilizer: liquid; bloodmeal and bonemeal
- water

WHAT TO DO

Choose a spot in early spring to make a garden bed for your strawberries. They grow well in a sunny position where the soil is well drained and not always soggy.

Dig the bed by loosening the topsoil and adding any organic matter: old decaying leaves or any compost you have made in your bin (see Winter, A Worm Farm, page 122).

Sprinkle over some fertilizer: a cupful of bloodmeal and bonemeal will get strawberries off to a good start.

Leave the bed for 1–2 weeks without planting. Allowing it to rest this way means you can dig out any weeds that grow.

Plant your runners 18 inches (45 cm) apart.

Water well and keep moist until the plants become established.

Feed the plants once a month with a fertilizer that dissolves in water, once your strawberry plants begin to flower. This will encourage the fruit to be large and sweet.

DID YOU KNOW?

? ? ? ?

If you have a lot of strawberries growing on 1 plant, they will be smaller in size than if you had only 1 or 2 strawberries growing. If you want really large fruit, pick off all but 2 flowers on each plant. The plant will then put all its energy into developing them and they will grow into 2 really big strawberries.

POTTING MIX

Use potting mix bought from a nursery or garden store when you are planting in pots. Soil from the garden will not be any good for growing potted plants because when watered it becomes compacted and no air will get to the roots of your plants. Roots need water, fertilizer and air. A good-quality potting mix will provide all of these for plants in a pot. The staff at your local garden store can advise you on the best one to buy.

GOOD-QUALITY POTTING MIX

- must be heavy enough to anchor the plant roots without being too heavy to handle
- must be able to be wet easily
- must not shrink and pull away from the sides of a pot
- must have enough space between the particles so air can get to the roots of a plant
- must be able to stay moist for a time, without becoming soggy
- must be free from weeds

From Flower to Fruit

Do you know where fruits come from? They develop from flowers. After a flower has been pollinated, the pollen moves down into the ovary. The pollen may then fertilize the ovules: a seed begins to form and the ovary grows and swells to form a fruit. The fleshy part of the fruit protects the newly formed seed inside.

♦♦♦

Fill a strawberry pot with potting mix and plant runners in the pockets and at the top. Water and fertilize regularly; place your pot in a sunny position and you can grow delicious strawberries. Watch that the birds don't get to them before you do!

♦♦♦

♦ *Make any extra strawberries into jam. It is delicious and easy to cook in the microwave.* ♦

Have you ever wondered why birds like eating your red fruit and vegetables, such as tomatoes and strawberries?

Red is a common color for ripe fruit for an important reason. Over many thousands of years, plants have made their ripe fruit a red color to attract birds and animals: birds and animals love the color red, and plants need creatures to eat their fruit. The fruit opens up inside the stomach and the seeds are released. The seeds then pass through the digestive tract and out in the animal's manure. In this way, new baby plants grow and the plant species will not become extinct.

Animals and birds are a plant's survival helpers. By turning its fruit from green to red when ripe, the plant is saying to its survival helper: 'Hey, my seed is ready to grow. Come and get it!'

What do you think would happen if the fruit stayed green?

Birds and animals wouldn't see the green fruit hidden among the green leaves and even if they did, they wouldn't be bothered trying to eat it because they prefer the color red.

Red is a color not seen by insects, which are too small to eat, digest, and distribute the seed. However, it is attractive to birds and animals that are big enough to be survival helpers by eating and excreting the seed so new little plants will grow.

Strawberry Jam

YOU WILL NEED

- 25 medium-sized strawberries
- 2 teaspoons fresh lemon juice
- 1½ cups (330 g) sugar
- a very large microwave-safe bowl
- microwave-safe plastic wrap
- a wooden spoon
- clean glass jars with lids
- a ladle
- labels

WHAT TO DO

Wash your strawberries. Take off the leafy tops, then cut the strawberries in half.

Place the pieces in the bowl, then add the lemon juice.

Cover with plastic wrap and cook in the microwave on HIGH (100% power) for 5 minutes. Remove from the microwave.

Stir in the sugar, return to the microwave and cook, uncovered, on HIGH for 5 more minutes. Stir the mixture, then cook for a further 3 minutes.

Ask an adult to ladle the hot mixture into hot, clean, dry jars. Place the lids on tightly while the jam is hot.

Make labels for the jars and glue them on once the jam has cooled.

IS A STRAWBERRY A BERRY?

Strawberries are not berries at all. Berries are fruit formed from a single ovary. Oranges are berries, as are all the citrus fruits. Tomatoes, pumpkins, watermelons, and bananas are also berries! A strawberry develops from many separate ovaries in the one flower, which means it is an aggregate fruit.

Be a Flower Hunter

Wandering around the garden and picking flowers is great fun. Do it in spring and summer when blossoming is at its peak and flowers are abundant.

Careful picking won't harm the plants and you will have great bunches of flowers for crafts or to arrange in a vase for your room.

Flowers look beautiful and smell wonderful.

Fun Flower Ideas

- Make a flower seller's stand.
- Arrange flowers in a vase for your room or for a centerpiece on the dinner table.
- Make a float bowl by filling a shallow dish of water with flowers having very short stems or no stems at all.
- Make a bouquet and tie it up with ribbon to give to a special friend, teacher, or family member for a surprise.
- Make a daisy chain or frangipani lei for a fragrant necklace.
- Make a fragrance trail. Go through your garden from one plant to another to find as many different perfumed flowers as you can.
- Press and use flowers in craft activities (see Spring, Flower Craft, page 30).
- Tie bunches of flowers together with string

and hang them upside down to preserve and dry (see Spring, Flower Craft).

- Pull petals from roses, lavender, or other fragrant flowers to make potpourri (see Spring, Flower Craft).
- Bring flowers inside and sort them into categories. Can you see any similarities or differences? Look at their color, the flower shape, the number of petals, and their size, and how many individual flowers are on the stem—one or many?
- Bring a flower inside and take it apart. What is it made up of? Can you see the petals, stamens, stigma, style, ovary, and calyx?

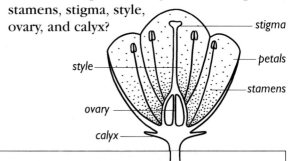

stigma

petals

stamens

style

ovary

calyx

DID YOU KNOW?

Many plants will bloom better and for a longer time if you pick their flowers.

Cutting off the older flowers is called deadheading because you are taking away the heads of the fading, dying flowers. Normally, when the floral parts die, a plant then turns its attention to producing seed within the flower. By removing the dying flowers, the plant's energy is moved from making the seed into making new growth and more flowers!

Making Flowers Bloom!

Each plant species has its own special time of the year to flower. Plants are amazing—some of them actually know when to flower because of the number of hours of light in the day!

In autumn and winter, when there are more hours of dark than light, chrysanthemums and poinsettias sense that it is time for them to flower. They are called short-day plants.

In spring, when days become longer, with more than 12 hours of light, plants such as hollyhocks and gladiolus respond and flower. They are called long-day plants.

Tricks can be played on plants to fool them into flowering out of their normal time. They can be grown inside and exposed to extra artificial light after nightfall. Or, you can make it dark for longer periods by closing the curtains during the day. Florists bring us beautiful flowering plants out of season, using this method of "forcing" flowers. Why don't you try it?

YOU WILL NEED

- a young chrysanthemum plant in a pot in spring or summer, that is not yet flowering
- a space inside a room that has curtains
- a space outside for your plant during the day

WHAT TO DO

Keep the pot in a darkened room in the afternoons and at night. Chrysanthemums need more hours of dark than light to flower.

Take the pot outside every morning and leave it in the light for about 6 hours.

Bring the plant inside again at about 3 o'clock every day.

Does the plant begin to flower? Of course for it to flower, you will have to look after it in other ways too: remember to water and fertilize.

When you have masses of flowers in your garden, pick some and arrange them in baskets and buckets like a flower shop. Add a cash register, toy money, handbags, and dress-up clothes to have hours of fun playing florists.

❖❖❖

GARDENING TIP

TIPS FOR CUTTING FLOWERS

- Use safety scissors to avoid accidents.
- Cut flowers early in the morning or late in the afternoon, when they are at their best.
- Take a small bucket of water with you; plunge the flowers straight in and they will last longer.
- Cut the stems on an angle to keep flowers fresher.
- Some flowers bruise easily, such as gardenias, roses, and hibiscus. Be careful not to touch the petals when picking these.
- When arranging flowers in a vase, remove any leaves that are under water. The water will stay pure longer.

29

Flower Craft

Flowers picked from your garden can be preserved by being pressed or dried. Once preserved, they can be stored in a dry, airy place. They will last for a long time and can be used when needed for craft activities.

Pressing Flowers

Pick flowers from your garden and you can press them to use in craft activities: pictures, collages, bookmarks, cards, or gift tags. Some flowers press more successfully than others. Roses, violets, hydrangeas, gerberas, pansies, and anemones give good results. Don't forget leaves, as they press quite easily. Both green leaves and colored autumn leaves are useful in pressed flower pictures. Leaf skeletons and some flat seed pods, such as honesty, and even grass seeds make interesting additions.

Pressed flowers are useful for making birthday and Christmas cards for your friends and family.

❖❖❖

CRAFT TIP

If you do not have a flower press, simply place your cut flowers in between several layers of newspaper and lay some heavy books on top. Change the paper every second day until your blooms are flat and dry.

YOU WILL NEED

- ◆ access to flowers and leaves
- ◆ safety scissors
- ◆ a basket for collecting flowers and leaves
- ◆ a flower press

WHAT TO DO

Collect flowers and leaves when they are at their driest.

Choose the best flowers. If they have been chewed by caterpillars or are beyond their peak and faded, pass them by. When you have made your selections, bring them inside.

Place the flowers carefully on the flower press, making sure the petals are not bent or squashed.

Layer the paper and flowers until all your material is in place.

Screw the lid on firmly but not tightly. Pressing the flowers in this way, draws moisture out of the flowers into the paper, so change the paper regularly to obtain good results. Change the paper every second day, to start, until your blooms are quite flat and dry; later extend the time to twice a week.

◆ Flowers, tied in bunches, hanging upside down to dry. ◆

Drying Flowers

Dry roses, lavender, hydrangeas, paper daisies, and statice by tying in bunches with string and hanging them upside down in a dry, airy spot.

Potpourri

YOU WILL NEED

- 2½ cups (125 g) dried petals of scented flowers or aromatic leaves
- ½ cup (25 g) orrisroot powder (available at health food stores)
- ¾ teaspoon (4 ml) essential oil (rose or lavender)
- 1 tablespoon ground cinnamon
- 1 cinnamon stick
- 12 cloves
- a large jar
- a small bowl
- a metal spoon for mixing
- a pretty bowl

WHAT TO DO

Place the dried petals and leaves in a large jar.

Set aside 1 tablespoon orrisroot powder. Sprinkle the remainder over the petals and leaves.

Blend 1 tablespoon orrisroot powder with essential oil in a small bowl. Add the mixture to the jar and mix well with the spoon.

Add the cinnamon stick and cloves; mix thoroughly. Place the potpourri in a pretty bowl.

31

Skip to My Lou

An expanse of lush green lawn is a perfect place to take a rope and practice your skipping. Using an individual rope, see how many ordinary skips or peppers (quick skips) you can do. Skipping on one leg, crossing the rope over when bringing it down or skipping by turning the rope backward are other variations. Don't stay in one spot, try running skipping! It is even more fun when you gather your friends around for a skipping session. Using a long rope, you might like to play some of the following games.

Skipping Games and Chants

Coming into and getting out of the turning rope is often the hardest part. Try the following chant while you practice:

Fish, fish come into the dish

(run in)

(skip the allotted number of times)

(run out)

Fish, fish go out of the dish

Once you have mastered getting in and out of the turning rope, you can add actions while skipping:

PUSSY CAT, PUSSY CAT, TURN AROUND *(do a 180° turn)*

PUSSY CAT, PUSSY CAT, TOUCH THE GROUND *(touch the ground with your hand)*

PUSSY CAT, PUSSY CAT, LIFT YOUR PAW *(hop on one leg)*

PUSSY CAT, PUSSY CAT, SKIP NO MORE *(run out)*.

*Skipping rope will test
your stamina and endurance.*

◆◆◆

⊥ When you have mastered these exercises and want to try Red Hot Peppers (quick skips) with the long rope, use this chant:

**Mabel, Mabel,
set the table
Bring the plates
if you are able
Don't forget the salt and
RED HOT PEPPER!**

On the words red hot pepper, turn the rope as fast as possible until the jumper misses.

Babies, babies at the gate
Eating biscuits from a plate
How many biscuits
did they eat?
One, two, three . . .

⊥ When taking turns in long-rope skipping, see how many skips your friends can reach before missing. Two chants for counting the number of skips are:

Bulldog, poodle,
bow wow wow
How many doggies
have we now?
One, two, three . . .

33

One Potato, Two Potato, Three Potato, Four!

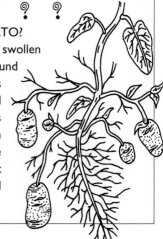

⊥ Raise a crop of potatoes by planting a potato that has gone to seed. There is no hard digging in this activity and one plant, well looked after will yield a good nest of delicious, healthy potatoes

Decorate your pot before planting takes place and it will make an interesting feature in the garden. Once you have planted your potato pieces, look after them by watering them regularly. They will grow into a shrubby plant and produce white or pale violet flowers. In 4–5 months from planting, turn your pot upside down and find the potatoes on the roots of the plant.

♦♦♦

Growing a Potato

YOU WILL NEED

- a potato
- a knife
- a saucer
- a dark place

WHAT TO DO

Cut the potato into several pieces with at least one eye on each piece (ask an adult to do this for you). The eye is a small hole on the surface of the potato and this is where the potato will send out shoots. Can you see them?

DID YOU KNOW?

? ? ? ?

WHAT IS A POTATO?

A potato is a tuber or swollen part of an underground stem. The tuber's job is to hold any extra food the plant makes, which is used by the plant when needed. The eyes of the potato are buds that send out shoots and grow into new plants.

Lay the pieces on a saucer and place the saucer in a dry, airy, dark spot.

Check your potato pieces every week or so. In time, the eyes will form buds that will then shoot. When the shoots are about 4 inches (10 cm) long, they are ready to be planted.

Plant your potato pieces outside in your no-dig garden.

Making a No-dig Garden

YOU WILL NEED

- a very large plastic pot (at least 20 inches [51 cm], diameter × 22 inches [56 cm] deep)
- well-aged lawn clippings or straw
- compost (see Winter, A Worm Farm, page 122)
- fertilizer: pelletized poultry manure or blood-meal and bonemeal
- newspaper

WHAT TO DO

Ask an adult to cut out the bottom of the pot.

Place the pot in a sunny position out in the garden.

Put a thin layer of newspaper (3–4 sheets) at the bottom of the pot and cover with a layer of straw and a layer of compost. You can also use decayed leaves.

Sprinkle a good handful of fertilizer over the layers.

Continue making these layers until the pot is filled.

Make small holes in the top of the materials; plant your potato pieces and cover them up again.

Harvest your potatoes in 4–5 months: turn your pot upside down and remove the potatoes from the roots of the plant.

Potato Printing

You can make attractive wrapping paper for birthdays or Christmas, cards, book covers, and decorations using potato prints.

YOU WILL NEED

- a potato
- a knife
- a scratching tool (pencil, nail file)
- paper towels
- nontoxic paint
- paper

WHAT TO DO

Ask an adult to cut the potato in half.

Scratch your design into the flat, cut surface of the potato with a scratching tool, to a depth of about ⅛ inch (3 mm).

Press the potato onto the paper towels to absorb excess moisture.

Dip the potato into the paint, being careful not to make the paint too thick.

Press onto the paper to make a print.

Twisting and Twining

Climbers are plants having long floppy stems that will grow upward on supports, or trail over fences or walls. Climbers are very interesting because they have different ways of getting to where they want to grow. Some have little roots along their stems that cling to a support; others have sucker pads like small feet that do the same thing. Others twine their stems around and around a pole or another plant. Some have tendrils to twine. Others have hooks or prickles that grab any support they can.

Growing Passion Fruit

Passion fruit grows on a vine that clings onto its support with tendrils. Passion fruit vines are fabulous to grow because they have attractive leaves, pretty flowers, and delicious summer fruit. Why don't you try growing one if you have space? You can buy a small plant from the nursery or raise your own vine by planting a seed from a store-bought passion fruit. When you grow a new plant from a seed, as described below, it is called propagating.

YOU WILL NEED

- a passion fruit, bought from the supermarket in spring
- a small pot
- potting mix
- water
- a warm, sheltered spot to grow the seedlings
- a spot in the garden, as the plant's permanent position

WHAT TO DO

Cut open the fruit and collect some seeds.
Wash all the pulp off and dry them.
Fill the pot with potting mix and press down firmly, leaving a ½ inch (1 cm) space at the top of the pot.
Water the mix.
Place your seeds in the pot.
Cover with ¼ inch (6 mm) of the mix and then water again.
Place in a warm, sheltered spot and keep the mix just moist. When the seeds germinate and the seedlings are 6 inches (15 cm) high, they are ready to plant.
Choose the strongest seedling.
Plant it into its permanent position. Vines will bear fruit from the second year onward, and when grown from seed, should live and bear well for 3–5 years.

GARDENING TIP

- Choose a frost-free, sunny spot in the garden to plant passion fruit.
- Have a strong support for it to grow on.
- Rich soil with free drainage is best.
- Water your plant well while it is growing.
- Replace your vines every 3–5 years.

Passion Fruit Ice Cream

Passion fruit ice cream, yummy!

YOU WILL NEED

- 2⅓ cups (600 ml) heavy whipping cream
- a 14-ounce (400 g) can of sweetened condensed milk
- ½ cup (125 ml) fresh lemon juice
- pulp of 3 passion fruit
- 2 large mixing bowls
- a hand electric mixer or a wire whisk
- a sharp knife
- a spoon
- a rubber spatula
- a lemon juicer
- a plastic container with a lid, for freezing

WHAT TO DO

Pour the cream into one of the mixing bowls and beat with the electric mixer (or wire whisk) until thick, and soft peaks form when the beaters are lifted out of the bowl.

Combine the condensed milk, lemon juice, and passion fruit pulp in the other mixing bowl.

Fold in the cream gently until it is all combined.

Spoon the mixture into the plastic container, cover with the lid, and freeze for several hours or until completely frozen.

Scoop the ice cream into bowls or cones to serve.

Note: This ice cream will keep in the freezer for 3 weeks.

◆ *Scoop out the passionfruit pulp and seeds to use in ice cream.* ◆

DID YOU KNOW?

The stems of twining climbers are thought to wind around clockwise in the Southern Hemisphere and counterclockwise in the Northern Hemisphere. Is this true? Check the twining plants in your garden and see what you find. Remember, twining climbers are those with stems curling around and around a support.

Halloween

Halloween is an autumn festival celebrated on October 31. Halloween has become an occasion of festivity, especially for children. Dressing up in a scary costume, playing trick or treat and collecting candy in return, and bobbing for apples are some of the activities associated with Halloween. Jack-o'-lanterns (Halloween lanterns) are also a familiar part of the present-day celebration.

Jack-o'-lantern (Halloween Lantern)

If you have grown pumpkins in your vegetable patch, you might like to save one for Halloween. Or, if pumpkins are sold in your area, you might find one suitable for carving a jack-o'-lantern.

Carving a jack-o'-lantern requires the use of sharp tools, so you will need an adult to help you with this activity.

YOU WILL NEED

- a pumpkin
- a sharp knife
- a spoon
- a felt pen
- a candle

WHAT TO DO

Ask an adult to carefully cut out the top of the pumpkin with a sharp knife.

Scoop out the seeds and scrape the flesh inside with a spoon.

Outline the eyes and mouth with a felt pen.

Carve a grinning face into the pumpkin, following the outline.

Put a candle inside; light it at night and place the lid on top of the pumpkin. Watch Jack's mischievous face glow!

◆◆◆
*Glowing jack-o'-lantern
ready for Halloween*
◆◆◆

Growing Pumpkins

Pumpkins grow on a rambling vine with large leaves and will use a lot of space in your plot. It will take 16–20 weeks, depending on the variety, to grow a pumpkin from seed.

Plant seeds outdoors when air temperature in spring stays about 60°F (16°C) during the day. If you have short summers, soak seeds overnight before planting.

FOR TRANSPLANTS YOU WILL NEED

- pumpkin seed (collect it yourself from a pumpkin or buy it in a packet from a plant nursery)
- potting mix
- a large peat pot
- water
- a plastic bag
- a garden tie or rubber band
- fertilizer: bloodmeal and bonemeal or soluble
- a warm, sunny spot in your vegetable garden

WHAT TO DO

Pumpkins do not transplant well and should be seeded outdoors if at all possible. If not, place in good-sized peat pots and transplant pots and all.

◆ *Planting pumpkin seeds in pots.* ◆

Leave the pot in a warm spot until the seedling emerges. When the seedling has grown 2 leaves, it is ready to be transplanted.

Plant the seedling still in the peat pot, in your vegetable patch.

Water regularly, especially in dry weather.

Fertilize monthly with bloodmeal and bonemeal or a soluble fertilizer, once the plant begins flowering and while it is bearing fruit.

Leave the fruit on the vine until it is fully mature.

Harvest when the vine dies and the fruit stalk turns brown and withers.

Note: When cutting the pumpkin off the vine, leave about 4 inches (10 cm) of the stalk attached to the fruit and it will keep better.

GARDENING TIP

When growing a pumpkin especially for Halloween, be sure to choose a cultivar that is appropriate for making a jack-o'-lantern. A firm pumpkin is better than one that rots quickly. The shape is also important: choose a round shape over a pear shape. Orange-skinned varieties are favorites but those with gray–green skin are just as good. Size does not matter: smaller ones are actually quicker to carve. Check descriptions on seed packets to find a suitable variety or ask the plant nursery staff for asssistance.

S U M M

Garden Discovery in Summer

In many regions, the heat of the summer can be strong. Avoid over-exposure to the sun and wear a hat and sunscreen for protection, whether exploring, climbing trees, playing with sand and water, digging beds, or tending plants.

Summer is a season when the garden is alive with the call of birds, the buzz of cicadas, and the chirping of crickets. Electrical storms with thunder and lightning may occur, giving a boost of growth to plants and trees. During these storms, lightning creates such energy that nitrogen, needed for plant growth, is produced.

• • •

By summer, you will be able to harvest some of the vegetables planted in spring.

• • •

Buzzy Bees

Bees may be regular visitors to your garden. They are good insects and important pollinators. They transfer the pollen from male flowers to female flowers. This may fertilize the female flower, which in turn enables the ovary of the flower to develop and swell into a fruit. Fruit and vegetable crops flourish because of bees.

• Make a bee from a balloon: let it go and it will fly around your garden! •

Buzzy Bees

You could make your own buzzy bee out of a balloon. Does it sound the same as a real bee when it moves? Real bees make a buzzing noise by vibrating their wings very quickly.

YOU WILL NEED

- a yellow balloon
- a thick black felt pen
- cellophane
- safety scissors
- adhesive tape

WHAT TO DO

Blow up the balloon and ask a friend or helper to hold the neck while you draw thick black rings around it.

Draw in some eyes and a mouth.

Cut out a large rectangle of cellophane and twist it in the middle to make wings. Tape the wings onto the top of the bee.

Let go of the bee and watch it buzz around in the air. You could blow up several balloons so that the garden is full of bees!

Bee Facts

Bees live in most parts of the world except for the North and South Poles. In a bee community, the queen is the leader. The male bee, or drone, has no sting and makes no honey. The female bees do all the work in the hive.

Bees are attracted by brightly colored and scented flowers. Flowers with bright blue or yellow petals are most likely to be seen and pollinated by bees. Bees don't see the color red, therefore red flowers are not pollinated by bees. Bees see ultraviolet light that people can't see.

Summer Painting Fun

For those fun and wonderfully messy painting activities, set up an old table or easel in the garden with paper, paints, brushes, and water. You could also tape a large sheet of paper to the fence for large-scale pictures or group work. Paintings don't take long to dry on hot summery days—hanging them by clothespins on the clothesline, to avoid a mess, is a good idea.

You can make lots of prints with finger paint.

♦ ♦ ♦

Finger Paint

YOU WILL NEED

- ½ cup soap flakes
- 6 cups (1.5 l) water
- 1 cup (250 ml) liquid starch
- food coloring or powdered tempera paint

WHAT TO DO

Dissolve the soap flakes in a little of the water until no lumps remain.

Add the starch and remaining water; mix well.

Add powdered tempera color or food coloring to make the paint vibrant.

Place blobs of the made-up finger paint on an old table or flat surface. Run your fingers and hands through, feeling and moving the paint around on the table.

Press your painty hands onto a clean sheet of paper to make hand prints. You could also experiment by creating patterns or drawing designs with your fingers.

Lay a sheet of paper over your finished pattern to make a print. Hang it up to dry.

YOU COULD ALSO

- Add sand, sawdust, or crayon shavings to the finger paint to add extra texture to a picture and to change the feel of the paint.
- Use a comb, fork, stick, notched cardboard, sponges, twigs, or leaves, instead of your hands and fingers, to create interesting designs and effects.

◆ Swirl, swirl, swish, swish—move the finger paint over the table. ◆

Try These Painting Ideas

BODY PAINTING

Great in summertime—hose off in the garden when you've finished.

FEET PRINTS

Lay out a long piece of paper and place a tray of nontoxic paint in front of it. Step into the tray, then walk along the paper.

SPLATTER PAINTING

Place a sheet of paper in a grassy area where paint splashes will not be a problem. Using thick brushes and watery paint, make a splatter design by flicking the brush over the paper.

SPRAY PAINTING

Water down some tempera or poster paint and pour it into a clean plastic spray container. Squeeze the trigger to squirt out jets of paint onto a piece of paper. Turn the nozzle to make a fine spray or a straight jet.

ROLLER PAINTING

The sponge on the roller gives a more even coverage of paint than does a brush. Use rollers to quickly cover background areas on large paintings. Rollers are available at hardware stores or in the paint section of department stores.

PRINTING

Using thick poster paint, print patterns with sponges, corks, cardboard shapes, old spools of thread, clothespins, toilet paper rolls, and other interesting bits and pieces.

BUBBLE PAINTING

Mix 1 cup (250 ml) of water with a squirt of liquid detergent and several drops of food coloring in a bowl. With a straw, blow into the mixture until colored bubbles form on the top. Quickly place a piece of paper over the top of the bubbles to make a print.

STRAW BLOWING

Place several little pools of different food dyes on a piece of paper. Point the end of a straw at the pools of dye and blow in the direction you want the dye to move. Try blowing one pool into another to blend colors and to create interesting patterns.

SPONGE PAINTING

Dampen a piece of paper with water. Cut pieces of moist sponge into small cubes; dip them into nontoxic paint and use like a brush to create a picture.

♦♦♦

*Get together with friends
to paint a mural. Tape a large sheet of paper
onto a fence where a few splashes and spills
will not matter.*

♦♦♦

CRAFT TIP

Painting need not be limited to a picture on paper. When you have the garden at your disposal, you can undertake bigger jobs. Keep any spare cardboard cartons and shoe boxes. Take them outside and paint them. They can become colorful hideaway houses, shops, city skyscrapers, cars, boats, and trains. Hang old sheets on the clothesline and paint murals on them. You can also paint tree branches that have been cut down or other pieces of wood and use them later for building and woodwork activities.

FENCE MURAL

Tape a long, large sheet of heavy paper securely onto a fence. Using sprayers filled with watery paint or rollers and thick paint, make a life-size picture with your friends.

WATERCOLOR PAINTING ON DAMP PAPER

Soak a piece of paper in water. Lay the paper on a table and smooth out all wrinkles. Using watercolors and a brush, paint directly onto the damp paper. Start with light colors first and leave the darker colors until last. The colors will mingle and blend into soft, fuzzy shapes. Experiment with the effects you can create. You will have to work fairly quickly before the paper dries.

WATERCOLOR WAX RESIST

Using a candle or wax crayon, draw a picture on your paper. Paint a color wash over your drawing using watercolor paint, applying the paint with a thick brush or a sponge. Experiment to discover and create interesting textures and effects.

From Seed to Tree

You can collect many seeds at home in the kitchen that will grow into trees. After you have eaten a piece of fruit, keep the seed. You could use orange, lemon, mango, or avocado seeds (suitable for warmer climates) and apple pips or any of the stone fruits (suitable for colder climates).

Grow a Peach Tree

After you have eaten a peach, you could grow a tree from its seed. After you have eaten all the fleshy part of the fruit, you will be left with a large stone. This is not the seed; it is a stone. This is a hard case that holds the seed inside to protect it. In nature, the stone would eventually split open or disintegrate and the seed would then be able to germinate. However, if you plant the seed without the hard outer casing, it will germinate quicker.

YOU WILL NEED

- a peach seed (break open the stone to get to the seed)
- a small pot
- potting mix
- water

WHAT TO DO

Place potting mix in the pot, leaving a ¾-inch (2 cm) space at the top.
Firm down and water.
Place the seed on the mix in the middle of the pot.
Cover the seed with mix to a depth of about ½ inch (1 cm). As a general rule, cover the seed with mix to a depth of twice its diameter. Press down firmly.
Water gently.
Place in a sunny position and keep moist until the seed germinates and grows.

DID YOU KNOW?

A peach fruit is called a drupe. A drupe is a fruit with an outer layer of skin, a fleshy middle, and a hard inner shell or stone. It usually has only one seed. Other drupes are cherries, nectarines, plums, almonds, apricots, avocados, coconuts, and olives.

♦ ♦ ♦
From peach to peach tree.
♦ ♦ ♦

peach

opened peach

peach stone

Seed Leaves and True Leaves

The seed leaves, cotyledons, are curled up tightly inside a seed, ready to emerge when germination takes place. When a seed begins to sprout and grow a stem, the seed leaves come out first, before any real leaves. They contain a store of food that the seedling can live off for a short time until the first true leaves grow. The true leaves will then produce food for the plant through photosynthesis.

leaves

seed leaves (cotyledons)

seed

stem

root

opened stone

seedling

young peach tree

Life Cycles

⊥ Different bugs and insects have their different life cycles. The garden offers an opportunity to observe many creatures at close range during the phases of their lives. In summer, adult insect activity is at its peak.

The Life of a Butterfly

Few insects change as much during their lives as the butterfly. A butterfly begins life as an egg that hatches into a caterpillar. The caterpillar hungrily eats leaves of plants, which annoys gardeners very much! It grows quickly and matures. The caterpillar then makes itself a snug home (chrysalis) and goes into the resting or pupal stage. The caterpillar is said to be resting because it is not feeding, but actually, a lot of activity goes on in the chrysalis. Great changes take place: the body of the caterpillar breaks down, reorganizes itself and transforms into a butterfly. It breaks free from its chrysalis, emerging as an adult butterfly, ready to fly and lay eggs, beginning the cycle over again.

When you see a butterfly in the garden, you might like to catch it in a butterfly net, being very careful not to harm it. Examine it closely and then let it go. You could also collect a caterpillar from the garden. Make a home for it in a box punched with air holes. Give it leaves to chew, and spray water inside the box to keep its home moist. You may be lucky enough to see it form into a chrysalis and emerge as a butterfly.

◆ *Life cycle of a butterfly.* ◆

D A N G E R !

   ⊠

When looking for insects in the garden, take care. Spiders are not insects, they are arachnids and a few of them are very dangerous. Although their webs are beautiful to look at, it is best not to touch spiders themselves.

Watching Butterflies

Observe butterflies in your garden:

- Do they fly alone or in groups?
- Where do they feed? What do they feed on? How do they feed?
- Are they in your garden in one particular season or are they there all the time?
- Does any animal attack them?
- How do they camouflage themselves to hide from their enemies?
- Can they fly a long way or do they move only short distances?

Record your observations in a notebook: you might discover a pattern to their behaviors. Look for other evidence of butterflies in your garden, such as small eggs on leaves that might turn into caterpillars, or a chrysalis that might have a butterfly inside.

Butterfly Blotter Art

YOU WILL NEED

- paper
- thick nontoxic paint
- a spoon

WHAT TO DO

Drop spoonfuls of different colored paint on one half of the page.
Fold the paper in half and press firmly.
Open out to make a pretty butterfly.

Carefully catch a butterfly in the garden to examine it closely.
◆◆◆

51

YOU WILL NEED

- an egg carton
- safety scissors
- green nontoxic paint
- a paintbrush
- a pipe cleaner
- 2 plastic eyes
- glue
- a red felt pen

- 12 eucalyptus seed capsules or other small seed capsules or pods

WHAT TO DO

Cut the egg carton in half, lengthwise.

Paint one of the carton halves green and allow to dry.

Cut the pipe cleaner in half and poke each piece into the caterpillar's head for feelers.

Glue on the eyes.

Draw a mouth.

Insert the eucalyptus seed capsules or other seed pods on each side of the caterpillar for legs.

♦♦♦
*This creepy, crawly caterpillar
will not eat your plants.*
♦♦♦

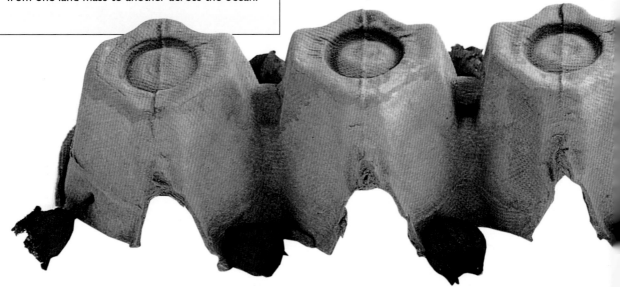

Plant Life Cycle

Just like people and animals, plants go through a cycle of life. In nature, they begin life as a seed produced by the parent plant.

When the seed ripens, it drops from the plant to the ground. Moisture softens the seed's outer coat and causes germination and growth. Roots reach down into the soil and shoots grow up into the air.

The new plant begins the juvenile stage of its life. It produces lush leafy growth. The plant matures into the adult stage of its life when it begins to flower and is capable of reproduction. When the plant's flowers are pollinated, fertilization can occur. The flowers then develop into fruit or cones. The fruit or cones produce seeds. The seeds ripen and fall onto the ground, and the cycle of life begins once again.

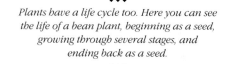

♦♦♦

Plants have a life cycle too. Here you can see the life of a bean plant, beginning as a seed, growing through several stages, and ending back as a seed.

♦♦♦

The Giant Gourd

A gourd is related to the pumpkin. Gourd fruits grow in many shapes, colors, and sizes. Some of them will grow to an enormous size—try planting one and beating the world record! The biggest gourd record to date is 108.1 pounds (49.04 kg). It was grown in California in 1990. The world record pumpkin was grown in 1992, in the state of Washington. It weighed 826.9 pounds (375.1 kg)!

◆ *Giant prizewinner pumpkin and ordinary pumpkins.* ◆

Discovery Activity

Plant an ordinary pumpkin and a prizewinner pumpkin. Look through seed catalogs to find pumpkins suited to your area. Compare and contrast them as they grow: leaf size, growth rate, plant spread. Then compare the size of the fruit that is produced by each plant. You will be surprised at the difference!

Note: If you have difficulty in finding prizewinner pumpkin seeds, try a specialist seed company or a rare seed supplier.

YOU WILL NEED

- seed, both large and normal cultivars
- a very large area with well-drained soil in a sunny spot
- plenty of water

WHAT TO DO

Follow the growing instructions for pumpkins (see Spring, Halloween, page 38).

Grow some seedlings according to the instructions on the packet.

Plant the seedlings in a prepared spot in the garden.

Water regularly, once the pumpkin plants are established. This will enable the fruit to grow to its biggest possible size.

Note: Removing all but a few of the pumpkins when they are small will cause the plant to put all its energy into developing them, resulting in even larger fruit.

◆◆◆
Look at the difference in size between a baby squash and a giant squash.
◆◆◆

OTHER GIANT PLANTS TO GROW

Search in seed catalogs for giant pumpkin, squash, or other large plants that grow in your area. You might find:

- New Guinea bean
- Giant Russian sunflower
- ordinary sunflower
- watermelon
- Big Max pumpkin
- Atlantic Giant pumpkin
- Prizewinner pumpkin
- Big Moon pumpkin

COOKING TIP

Pumpkin seeds can be eaten and are easy to roast at home. Ask an adult helper to cut open a pumpkin, then scoop out the seeds, and clean and dry them. Mix the seeds with a little salt and oil. Spread the seeds evenly on a tray and place in the oven; set at 350°F (180°C) for about 20 minutes. Cool, crack them open and remove the kernel, which you can eat. Pumpkin seeds are very good for you. They are full of nutrients and make a delicious and healthy snack.

Baby Vegetables

Small, plant varieties with tiny vegetables or fruit are easy to grow either in the vegetable plot or in pots. Tomatoes, pumpkin, cauliflower, lettuce, and carrots are some of the more popular vegetables that have small varieties. They are great fun to grow and a treat to eat!

Baby vegetables are good for small spaces. Grow some in pots.

• • •

Seed Supplies

Many seeds are available at plant nurseries or at the supermarket. If these exact varieties are not sold in your area, look for similar types. Someone at your local garden shop can help you. There are also some companies that sell all types of seeds. You can look at their lists and order seeds through the mail. (See page 8.)

LOOK FOR THESE SEED PACKETS

BEET	Golden Beet, Kestrel
CABBAGE	Rougette
CARROT	Thumbelina, Kinko
SWEET PEPPER	Jingle Bells
CAULIFLOWER	White Rock
SWEET CORN	Golden Midget
CUCUMBER	Early Russian Heirloom, Lemon
LEEK	Scotland Heirloom, King Richard
LETTUCE LITTLE GEM	Buttercrunch, Tom Thumb, Bronze Mignonette
WATERMELON	Garden Baby, Sugar Baby
PUMPKIN	Baby Bear, Jack-Be-Little, Small Sugar
SQUASH BUTTERCUP	Sweet Dumpling
TOMATO	Whipper Snapper, Sun Cherry, Washington Cherry, Gold Nugget, Yellow Pear
ZUCCHINI	Gold Rush, Condor

◆ *Baby carrots grown in pots and ready to eat.* ◆

Splish, Splash—
Cooling off Time

In the heat of the summer, playing with water in the garden is a cooling way to spend time. Remember, before you go out, slip on a T-shirt, smooth on sunscreen, and slap on a hat, to reduce overexposure to sun.

Water Games

WATER RACE

Give each player a plastic beaker full of water.
Start the race: on "go," everyone must run from one end of the garden to the other, trying not to spill any water. The winner is the one who gets to the end of the garden first, without spilling any.

FILL THE BUCKET

Place a very big bucket filled with water at one end of the lawn.
Give each player an empty plastic squeeze bottle to hold.
Place a large empty bowl at the other end of the lawn, opposite each player. All bowls and all plastic bottles should be the same size.
Start the race: on "go," the players will squeeze their bottle, holding the nozzle under water in the bucket to suck up water and fill their bottle. Then they will run to their bowl and squirt the water into it. They will run back and forth repeating this.
Stop the race after 2 minutes. The winner is the one with the most water in his or her bowl.

♦♦♦

*You can have lots of fun while you are
watering the garden. If your trees need water,
you could have an outdoor shower at the
same time. Put on your bathing suit, then hang
the hose in the tree and turn the water on.
You can have great fun under the cool
running water. You might use an umbrella.
How about wearing your goggles
and rain boots too?
Why not invite your friends over to cool off
and join in the fun?*

♦♦♦

GARDENING TIP

Water is a scarce resource and should be used carefully and not wasted. If water restrictions apply, take note of them. When playing games with a hose or sprinkler, stand where the water is most needed so the lawn, trees, or garden will get a drink at the same time. Avoid playing with hoses and sprinklers in the middle of the day—not only is the sun at its strongest and you may get sunburned but also the water will be lost in evaporation. After playing with a water container, don't tip the water down the drain—it can be scooped out in cupfuls for watering your potted plants.

◆ *Water fun out in the garden.* ◆

Water Container Fun for Toddlers

Place a trickling hose and play equipment into a water container or tub and have hours of enjoyment. Pouring, filling, and measuring with water are great fun. It is interesting to compare the capacity of different containers and also practice counting. How many spoonfuls of water make up a cup? How many cups of water would fill a pitcher? Guess before you measure and then see if you are right.

Try some of the following activities:

GAMES TO PLAY

◆ tipping and filling beakers and pitchers
◆ washing plastic dishes

60

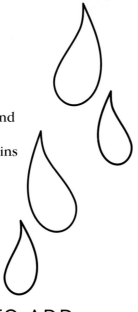

- sailing boats
- washing dolls clothes
- giving dolls a bath
- fishing with a toy rod and line and plastic fish
- fish, whales, and dolphins
- submarines
- harbor master: moving around toy boats, ferries, and tugboats

THINGS TO ADD

- food coloring to make colored water
- detergent to make bubbles
- plastic kitchen equipment: cup, spoon, ladle, sieve, funnel, pitcher, whisk, beater
- a clear plastic tube for funneling
- squeeze bottles to fill and squirt
- sponges
- corks
- plastic toys

DANGER !

Young children must be supervised when they are engaged in any water activity. Children can drown in shallow water, in small quantities of water, or in very small containers of water.

Wash and dry your doll's clothes on a nice sunny day.

♦♦♦

Beetles and Bugs

Wander around the garden and look carefully among the trees and bushes and on the ground: you will find a wide range of beetles and bugs. Ladybirds, beetles, grasshoppers, cockroaches, crickets, ants, and earwigs might inhabit your garden! Some bugs and beetles are nocturnal: that means they sleep during the day and come out to feed at night, so you might have trouble finding them. Others may be hard to see as a lot of beetles and bugs are the same color as the plants they feed on. They hide or camouflage themselves in this way so they are protected from animals that eat them.

The Life of a Cicada

The cicada is a bug with a very interesting life cycle. It starts life above ground, as an egg laid by a mother cicada in a tree.

When the egg hatches, the baby cicada emerges. It is called a nymph and is wingless. It drops out of the tree to the ground

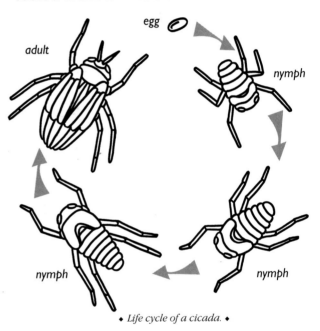

♦ *Life cycle of a cicada.* ♦

and burrows down into the earth where it spends most of its life.

After many months—or sometimes even years—underground, growing and maturing, the nymph moves upward out of the ground, climbs into a bush, and sheds its skin. To do this, a crack appears down its back and it squeezes out of its old skin. Once it emerges from its old skin, it spreads its new wings and flies up into the trees to lay eggs and start the cycle once again.

DID YOU KNOW?

❓ ❓ ❓ ❓

BEETLE AND BUG FACTS

- Beetles and bugs are insects. Spiders, centipedes, millipedes, earthworms, snails, and slugs are not.
- The hearing parts of crickets and grasshoppers are on the abdomen or forelegs.
- If a grasshopper loses a front leg, another leg grows in its place.
- Grasshoppers have such powerful hind legs that they can jump twenty times their own length.
- Beetles have the hardest armor of all insects.
- Bugs are crawling insects. They don't have teeth or chewing parts, but suck sap or juice through a proboscis on their lower lip.

Ladybird,
Ladybird,
Fly Away Home!

Ladybirds are beetles that you will find in the garden. They do a good job of eating aphids. Aphids are pests that do damage to plants, so look after ladybirds and they will keep the garden healthy. Try making a ladybird sculpture for fun.

YOU WILL NEED

- 4 slices of bread, crusts removed
- craft glue
- lemon juice, a few drops
- acrylic or tempera paint
- a paintbrush

WHAT TO DO

Tear the bread into small pieces.
Mix thoroughly with 3 tablespoons of craft glue and a few drops of lemon juice.
Model a ladybird or other beetle or bug.
Push in pipe cleaners for legs and round seeds glued to match sticks for feelers, if necessary for your particular bug. Plastic eyes may be used. Allow 1–2 days to dry.
Paint your ladybird or bug.
Note: The bread dough will keep for several days in a plastic bag in the refrigerator.

If you have cicadas in your region and can find any cicada shells in summer, examine them with a magnifying glass. What can you see? What do you think the split down the back of the shell might be?

•••

Happy Herbs

Making an herb garden is simple to do. Herbs are easy plants to look after and happily grow in pots or in the ground. When your herbs become established and begin to flourish, take pieces for cooking or for use in craft activities. Dry herbs for craft by hanging them upside down in bunches.

Make an herb garden in pots and place them in a sunny little nook outside. Look after your plants; water them when they are thirsty and soon you will have a group of happy herbs!

❖❖❖

Herbs in Pots

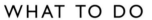

Lavender is a popular herb for potpourri.

YOU WILL NEED

- clay garden pots
- nontoxic paint to decorate pots (look for one that won't wash off)
- paintbrushes
- potting mix
- slow-release fertilizer
- a trowel
- water
- a watering can
- herb seeds
- labels for the plants (you can write the name of the plant on a popsicle stick and push it down into the side of the pot)

WHAT TO DO

Decorate your pots with paint. Allow to dry.

Place potting mix and some of the fertilizer granules into the pots, using the trowel, and press down firmly.

Water.

Sprinkle a little seed on the top of the mix.

Place a thin layer of potting mix on top of the seeds.

Press firmly and water again.

Add labels or you might forget which herb is in which pot.

Place your pots in a sunny position.

Keep moist and the seed will germinate and grow. Be sure to water regularly, as water will evaporate more quickly in pots than in the ground.

Note: If you are using very small pots, transplant into bigger ones when your herbs begin to grow. For full instructions, see Potting a Plant, page 91.

An Herb Garden

You will need to set aside a special plot for your herbs; ask an adult to help you prepare one in a sunny area. (Only a few herbs like shade—most prefer basking in the sun.) You could choose any shaped plot, but a circular one divided into sections is traditional.

Choose the herbs you wish to grow and buy seed packets. Simply mix the seed with a little sand and broadcast each different herb into a particular section of the plot. Water and keep moist during early growth.

GARDENING TIP

EASY-TO-GROW HERBS		HERBS FOR SUN		HERBS FOR SHADE
Parsley	Chives	Lavender	Nasturtium	Violet
Mint	Basil	Borage	Rosemary	Mint
Nasturtium	Lavender	Lemon verbena	Sage	Cress

Before planting, organize your herb garden by listing what you will need and what plants you will grow. Draw up a design. Any seed saved for this project can be kept in labeled envelopes until you are ready to sow.

Herbs for Potpourri

You can add some of the herbs you've grown to your homemade potpourri (see Spring, Flowercraft, page 30). The flowers and leaves of your herbs should be dried first before being used in potpourri. Fragrant seeds can also be an interesting addition. Here are some suggestions for herb leaves, flowers, and seeds that are ideal for use in potpourri:

- Leaves: rosemary, mint (peppermint), marjoram, thyme, sage
- Flowers: lavender, violet
- Seeds: caraway, angelica, coriander

Herb Crafts

Herbs can be used fresh for cooking. However for craft activities, dry your herbs first. Make lavender bags to scent your closet or underwear drawer or place herb potpourri in a bowl to add a fresh aroma to any room. For a relaxing night's sleep try making an herb pillow. Sweet dreams!

Drying Herbs

Sew pretty bags and fill them with dried lavender. Tie up with ribbon.

YOU WILL NEED

- herbs to pick
- string
- a drying rack
- a well-ventilated room

WHAT TO DO

Pick stems with foliage early in the morning, before the sun has reached the leaves.
Tie in bunches with string.
Hang upside down on a drying rack in an airy, well-ventilated room.

Sand Castles and Mud Pies

Take the opportunity during the warm summer weather to play with sand and water. If you have a sandbox in your garden, you can have hours of summer fun. If you don't have a sand-box, you can buy a bag of sand from a garden nursery and pour it into a large heavy plastic container (available at some supermarkets and most hard-ware stores). Add a trickling hose—sand is easier to mold and build with when wet.

Mud Roads

You can make mud in the garden by wetting some soil. When the soil is wet, press a thick piece of wood down into the mud. Move it along to form the smooth surface of a road. Leave the mud road to dry in the sun. When dry, you can drive your toy cars along it.

A container of sand is a good substitute for a sandbox in gardens with little space. Choose a sturdy plastic container, fill it with one or two bags of sand, and add some digging equipment and plastic bowls. You could also try making a mini-city with roads, toy cars, people, and cardboard buildings.

❖❖❖

The feel of mud is entirely different from that of wet sand: take the opportunity to mix dirt and water, and play around in the result! If space allows, have a dirt pit; if not, make mud pies and cakes in a small corner of the garden.

❖❖❖

A U T

Garden Discovery in Autumn

The cooler autumn weather comes as a relief after a long hot summer. It is a time when leaves color and drop—a spectacle to enjoy. Pad across a stretch of ground that is thickly and softly carpeted with leaves of brilliant colors. The flowers that were budding in spring have bloomed and are now going to seed. There will be plenty of dried pods and seeds to collect for craft activities.

Don't just be a spectator, play and work in the garden. The cooler weather is perfect for running and playing games in the garden or for serious digging and planting.

◆◆◆

Collect the leaves, examine them, and compare and contrast: use them for craft. They are also wonderful to compost!

◆◆◆

U M N

Letting off Steam

Autumn, with its crisp cool weather, is the perfect time to use the garden for run and fun games to get rid of excess energy and to warm you up. Invite some of your friends over to share your garden and join in the fun.

Tortoise and Hare

Choose someone to be the caller.
Creep around slowly when the caller says "Tortoise."
Run around as fast as you can when the caller shouts "Hare."

Statues

Run around.
Freeze in position on the command "Stop": on one foot, on hands and feet, bending over, or any other position.
Wobble or fall and you're out!

◆ *You will need strong muscles to win tug of war.* ◆

♦ Warm up by playing leapfrog with your friends. ♦

Obstacle Course

HERE ARE SOME IDEAS FOR YOUR OBSTACLE COURSE

- Place a plank of wood across two big, strong flowerpots. Use it as a balance beam to walk along and jump off.
- Tie a heavy rope to a sturdy tree branch; swing off it.
- Put a ladder against a fence to climb up and down or lay the ladder on the ground and take quick, tiny steps through the rungs.
- Lay hoops on the ground and jump from one to the other.
- Place jump ropes in one area for a skipping session.
- Put down large cardboard boxes with their tops and bottoms removed and use them as tunnels to crawl through.

DANGER !

Running an obstacle course will require adult supervision at all times.

Cat and Mouse

Pick two children from your group: one to be the cat and one to be the mouse. Have the rest of the children form a circle around the mouse by linking hands.

Protect the mouse inside the circle. The cat will be outside your circle. The cat has to try to get in through the linked hands and catch the mouse.

Let the mouse out at any time by raising your arms, but be quick so the cat can't follow.

Scavenger Hunt

Make a list of garden bits and pieces to find: leaf, feather, smooth stone, pine cone, bug, grass seed.

Run on the word "go" to find those things on the list. The first to collect them all is the winner.

YOU COULD ALSO PLAY

- Leapfrog
- Tag
- Follow-the-leader
- Hide and seek
- What's the time, Mr. Wolf?

Seed Search

Some plants bear seeds and some do not. Ferns, mosses, algae, and mushrooms are some of the plants you may be familiar with that do not reproduce by way of seed. Most of the plants in your garden will be flowering plants, which bear fruit containing seeds. Even grasses have flowers, although you may not have noticed them as they are tiny and green. Grass flowers bear a lot of seed. You may have seen conifer trees: they have cones rather than flowers and the cones hold their seeds.

GARDENING TIP

HOW TO COLLECT SEEDS

Examine the plants in your garden to see if they are carrying any dying flowers, ripening fruit, or seed pods. It is important to catch fruit at a stage before it is too ripe. If you wait until it is fully ripe, it may have already opened and dropped its seed.

Cover a dying flower or ripening fruit with a small plastic bag and tie it up with a twist tie. As the flower dies, it will swell to form the fruit. When the fruit ripens and opens, the seed it contains will fall into the bag. Collect the seeds once they have fallen into the bag.

Note: You may wish to observe the seed, compare it to other types you have collected, catalog it, or plant it.

Cataloging Seed

Make a special cardboard frame with cellophane windows—it is useful to keep and catalog any seeds you collect. You might be surprised how many different types of seed you can find in your own backyard. Compare your seeds. How are they different? How do you think each type might travel? (See Did You Know, page 74.)

YOU WILL NEED

- a sheet of cardboard
- clear cellophane
- safety scissors
- adhesive tape

♦♦♦
A flower pollinated by bees or other insects may become fertilized. The flower then turns into a fruit that has seeds inside.
♦♦♦

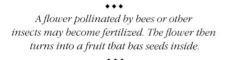

◆ It is great fun to play a game of helicopters with the winged seeds of maple trees. ◆

WHAT TO DO

Cut out squares of cellophane.
Mount the seeds on the cardboard and cover them with the cellophane squares.
Tape the edges of the cellophane to the cardboard.

There is a Plant Inside the Seed!

Look in your garden for some big seeds. The vegetable plot is a good place to start. Beans and peas have large seeds inside their pods. Broad beans and lima beans are especially big. The kernels on a corncob are also seeds and are big enough to use. Gather your seeds. Ask an adult to cut them in half lengthwise. You will see the beginnings of the baby plant inside. For dried seeds, soak overnight first.

◆◆◆

The beginnings of a baby plant inside the seed.

◆◆◆

SEEDS CAN TRAVEL

Seeds move in many different ways from their parent plant to a spot on the ground where they may germinate and grow into new plants.

The seeds of some trees, such as maples, have papery wings so they can travel on the wind to a faraway place. The wind can move dandelion seeds too, which have thin, threadlike hairs, similar to parachute lines, to help them drift further.

Other seeds explode from their pod, shooting out into the air. Touch a ripe Busy Lizzie (*Impatiens*) seed pod and see what happens!

Some seeds have special lightweight shells to help them travel in water. The coconut is a seed and its outer husk allows it to float over the seas from one island to another.

Animals and birds also help seeds to travel. They eat fruit with the seeds inside. The fruit opens inside their stomachs and the seeds come out in their droppings—instant fertilizer to get the seed off to a good start! When you consider how far birds fly, it is not difficult to imagine how populations of plants can travel from one place to another, quite a distance away.

Seeds can also be carried to their new home on people's skin or animals' fur. These seeds have tiny hooks attached to them that cling onto fur, clothes, and skin.

Papery wings of maple seeds spin around like helicopter blades as they fall to the ground.

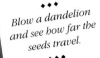

Blow a dandelion and see how far the seeds travel.

Seed Mosaic

The autumn garden will provide you with lots of seeds from flowering plants and vegetables that you can turn into creative pictures.

To make a seed mosaic, collect seeds from the fruit and vegetables you have eaten.

You could use seeds from pumpkins, apples, oranges, watermelons, apricots, and cherries.

You could also collect from flowers in the garden that have gone to seed. Use the same method as for collecting seed (see Autumn, Seed Search, page 72).

Dried corn kernels, rice, and wheat are also very useful.

Leave the seed its natural color or dye it with food coloring.

YOU WILL NEED

- cardboard
- craft glue
- a variety of seeds
- a small paintbrush

WHAT TO DO

Plan a design on the cardboard.

Paint the glue on one area of the design at a time.

Press the seeds into place.

Move to the next section once you have completed one area, until you have completed the design.

Note: Use tweezers for smallish seeds that are difficult to pick up. Really tiny seeds can be poured onto the glued area and the excess dusted off when the glue has dried.

◆ *Vegetable seed mosaic picture.* ◆

Hidden Creatures

Apart from the animals and insects living in your trees and shrubs and on the ground, there is a whole world of living creatures below your garden. To find out about your very own underground animals, do some soil sieving!

◆ *Wriggly worms live in soil.* ◆

Soil Sieving

YOU WILL NEED

- a dish
- soil from the garden
- a trowel
- a sheet of white paper
- a large sieve
- a magnifying glass
- paper and a pencil

WHAT TO DO

Collect a dish of topsoil from your garden, using the trowel. Can you see any hidden creatures yet? There might be some big ones such as earthworms.

Hold the sieve over the sheet of paper.

Add some of the soil and gently shake to separate the soil from the smaller animals.

Examine the paper and the sieve carefully when you've finished. How many different animals can you find? You may need to use the magnifying glass to see them.

Make a record of them. Draw the different types and count how many there are. Return the soil and the creatures to where they belong once you have finished.

Where Does Soil Come From?

Soil comes from rock that has weathered down and broken up into very small pieces. It takes many, many years for rock to become soil. Rock is full of minerals, and so soil also contains minerals that plants use as food. Plants can only take up these minerals, or nutrients, if they are dissolved in water, so moisture is very important to plants.

If you feel the top of the ground in your garden, you are probably not touching the soil minerals at all. There is usually organic matter—leaves, twigs, stems, fruit, and flowers of trees and plants—that has dropped and decayed. This top layer is called humus. It comes from something that was once living: organic. Soil minerals come from rocks that were not living and are said to be inorganic. The mineral part of the soil and the organic matter are mixed up with the help of our friends, the earthworms, to make a very good place for plant roots to live.

Leaves Are Falling Down

Autumn is a wonderful time for watching changes in the garden. It is especially interesting if you have trees and shrubs whose leaves change color from green to yellow, purple, red, brown, or orange in autumn and then fall, leaving the branches bare in winter. These trees and shrubs are called deciduous. Their leaves will grow back again in spring.

Seasonal Cycle

In autumn, the bottom of each leaf stem begins to harden. Less and less water passes from the twig into the leaf. The leaf begins to lose its green color. Chlorophyll in the leaves makes them green, but in autumn, less chlorophyll is being made because the light isn't as strong as in summer and because the days are becoming shorter. Different colors or pigments take over. While the leaves are dying, they turn yellow, red, purple, orange, or brown. Soon after these beautiful colors appear, the leaves die completely and fall to the ground. Sometimes they are helped by gusty autumn winds tearing the withered leaves from their branches. Any left on the tree will be pushed off by the new spring growth.

In spring, new leaves will be ready to take the place of the old ones. They are curled up tightly in buds, covered with thick coats. When the warmer weather comes in spring, sap (plant food and water) rises from the roots. Any food stored in the stems and branches is also released. With all this food now available, the buds swell, open, and grow. Out come the new leaves.

DID YOU KNOW?

❓ ❓ ❓ ❓

WHY DO SOME TREES LOSE THEIR LEAVES?

Some trees prepare for winter by shedding their leaves. This is a response built into trees over millions of years. Deciduous plants come from areas where winters are severely cold and the ground freezes. When moisture in the soil is frozen, a plant cannot take it up. So the trees adapted to the lack of water in wintertime by shedding their leaves. In their bare state, trees are dormant and do not need nearly as much water to survive as ones full of leaves.

Collecting Leaves

Autumn is the best time to start a leaf collection. When the leaves have fallen, simply pick them up off the ground.

YOU WILL NEED

- an assortment of autumn leaves
- several sheets of newspaper
- heavy books
- an empty scrapbook
- glue
- a pen or a pencil

WHAT TO DO

Collect as many different colored and different shaped leaves as you can.

Place your leaves between sheets of newspaper and put a few heavy books on top to flatten them out and dry them completely.

Sort the pressed leaves into groups and put all the similar types together.

Glue the leaves into a scrapbook.

Label any leaves you can identify with the names of the trees they fell off.

◆ *Throwing autumn leaves.* ◆

Autumn Art

⊥ The autumn season provides us with an abundance of natural craft materials. Red- and gold-colored autumn leaves, and all shapes and sizes of seed pods, seeds, and twigs can be crafted into collage pictures, seed pod sculptures, jewelry and ornaments. For two easy, fun activities using autumn leaves, try a sealed nature picture and splatter painting.

◆ *Brush paint over a sieve to make a splatter print.* ◆

Splatter Painting

YOU WILL NEED

- fallen autumn leaves or twigs and seed pods
- paper
- a kitchen sieve
- watery paint or food coloring
- a stiff brush or toothbrush

WHAT TO DO

Arrange the leaves (or twigs and seed pods) on a large sheet of paper.

Hold the sieve over the paper, dip the brush into the paint, and scratch the brush over the sieve.

Continue brushing until the splattered effect on the paper is of a suitable darkness.

Remove the leaves carefully and, with clothespins, hang up the painting to dry.

Sealed Nature Picture

YOU WILL NEED

- waxed paper
- colored leaves
- adhesive tape
- safety scissors
- an iron

WHAT TO DO

Cut two pieces of waxed paper of equal size.

Lay one sheet out and arrange your autumn leaves in a pattern.

Place the other waxed sheet over the first, covering the leaves.

Iron over the second sheet with a warm iron (ask an adult to do this for you). Ironing will seal the two sheets together, preserving the leaves in between the paper (the wax will not stick to the iron).

Tape the finished product onto your bedroom window and when the light streams through, your sealed nature picture will really glow.

◆ ◆ ◆
Preserve autumn leaves in waxed paper
◆ ◆ ◆

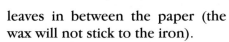

Leaf Skeletons

Just like people, leaves also have skeletons. In people, the skeleton is a frame to hold up, protect, and help move the body. In a leaf, it is a frame to support the leaf surface, and also is the network of veins that transports food through the plant.

Forage around on the ground under some large trees and you might be lucky enough to find a leaf skeleton. The blade of the leaf will have disintegrated by rotting or will have been eaten by insects, leaving only the skeleton remaining.

Skeleton Rubbing

YOU WILL NEED

- leaves
- paper
- crayons

WHAT TO DO

Place a leaf on a flat surface.
Position the paper over it and rub gently with the side of the crayon. The pattern of the leaf's veins will show up on the paper.

If you cannot find a leaf skeleton in your garden, try doing a skeleton rubbing.

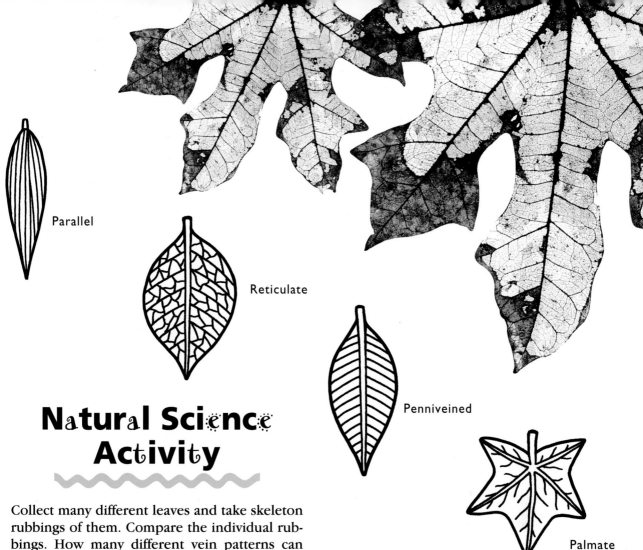

Parallel

Reticulate

Penniveined

Palmate

Natural Science Activity

Collect many different leaves and take skeleton rubbings of them. Compare the individual rubbings. How many different vein patterns can you find?

DID YOU KNOW?

LEAF FACTS

- Leaves come in all different shapes and sizes. Some leaves are huge. The leaves of the raffia palm can measure up to 65 feet (19. 8 m) in length.
- The leaves of many plants are poisonous. Rhubarb leaves are very toxic even though the stems are delicious stewed and made into desserts.
- Some leaves are used to make medicines. The poisonous leaves of the biennial foxglove (*Digitalis purpurea*) are processed to make the medicine digitalin,

used in treating heart conditions.
- The leaves of many plants have a strong and pleasant smell. Some are crushed to make an oil. When diluted, the oil is inhaled or rubbed into the skin. Lavender is said to be refreshing and relaxing, and eucalyptus is warming and antiseptic.
- Tea is made from the leaves of one of the camellia species, *Camellia sinensis*. Herbal tea is also made from leaves as peppermint or camomile.

Creative Hideaways

You needn't have a fancy hideaway or playhouse when you have a garden with secret spots and bushy alcoves. Explore your garden to find a suitable nook to create your own private place to play by yourself or with your friends. A spreading bush with its lower branches undercut is an ideal place for having a tea party or playing pirate coves. You could turn it into a dragon's lair or a fairy castle. Get some dress-up clothes, collect a few props, pack a picnic lunch to stop any stomach grumbles, and away you go!

YOU COULD ALSO

- Take a table outside and cover it with a large sheet, shower curtain, blanket, or tarpaulin and play underneath.
- Attach one or two large sheets to the lower branches of a tree, to form a tepee around the trunk.
- Set up a tent outside, if you have one.
- Use large boxes or packing crates to make the rooms of a house.
- Hang some sheets on the outside line of a circular clothesline, to make a cozy room within.
- Tack some sheets onto the rafters of a trellis to form an enclosure.

DID YOU KNOW?

Some ants that make their nests underground help farmers by breaking up the soil, loosening it, and mixing it.

The Ants Go Marching One by One...

Picnic in your hideaway and you might receive some unexpected guests, especially if you have sweet treats such as cookies! Ants are partial to sweet tastes, even though they eat a variety of food such as dead animal matter, other insects, seeds, and fungi. If you leave any sugary crumbs scattered around, you could find ants marching up one by one to take them away.

Why do you think ants behave like soldiers in a procession and march one behind the other?

Ants have a strong social structure, as do bees, with a queen, female workers, and males. They live in a nest or colony. The type of work done by each group in the colony is strictly divided. Some particular ants have the job of finding food. When a foraging ant locates food, it returns to the nest, leaving a trail of chemicals. This is like a "smell trail" that other ants can follow to reach the food source. The workers follow the trail, collect the food, and bring it back to the colony. They will feed the queen and her larvae with small pieces of the food.

◆ *Invite your friends to a tea party!* ◆

Beautiful Bulbs

⊥ The bulb part of a plant is a swollen stem, normally underground. Roots grow down from its flat base, and leaves and flowers grow upward from the narrow top of the bulb. The flowers and foliage die each year. The bulb can then be dug up and stored, ready to be replanted the following year.

Cuban lily bulbs in flower.

Make a potted bulb garden. In late autumn, place some peat moss (available from a plant nursery) or potting mix in the bottom of a pretty container, position a few bulbs on top, and cover with peat moss. Water a little when the peat moss feels dry. By spring, your bulbs will be growing and blooming. Bring them inside for a while to decorate your room.

♦♦♦

GARDENING TIP

SOME FAVORITE BULBS FOR YOU TO PLANT

BULB	FLOWER COLOR	PLANTING TIME	FLOWERING TIME
Daffodil	yellow	autumn	spring
Freesia	white, cream, purple	autumn	spring
Grape hyacinth	purple	autumn	spring
Hyacinth	pink, purple, white	autumn	spring
Jonquil	yellow, white	autumn	spring
Nerine	pink	summer	autumn
Ranunculus	red, yellow, white, orange	autumn	spring
Scarborough lily	red	spring	summer
Tulip	red, white, yellow, purple	autumn	spring

Windy Windy Is the Weather

Air is all around us, constantly moving. Sometimes air moves so slowly that you can barely feel it. It can move a little faster to form a gentle breeze or move quickly with great force, as in gusty storms.

Which Way Is the Wind Blowing?

YOU WILL NEED

- crepe paper
- safety scissors
- elastic
- a tree or place to hang the streamers

WHAT TO DO

Cut the crepe paper into 5 or 6 long ribbons, about 3 feet (1 m) in length.
Tie the ends to a length of elastic.
Knot the ends of the elastic together to form a hoop.
Place this stretchy hoop over a tree branch on a windy day.
Observe. You can tell which way the wind is blowing by watching the streamers move around.

YOU COULD ALSO

- Make a kite and fly it.
- Make wind chimes.
- Make a weather vane.
- Watch the washing on the line and see which way it's blowing.
- Watch leaves on the trees and gauge the wind direction from the way they are blowing.

DID YOU KNOW?

? ? ? ?

WIND AFFECTS PLANTS

Wind has a great effect on plants in many ways.

- It can either cool or warm a plant's surface, depending on the direction of the wind and the local temperature.
- Wind influences the amount of water a plant loses through transpiration and may even cause drying up of plant tissues during severe, hot gusts.
- Strong winds are likely to cause damage to leaves such as ripping or shredding.
- In exposed areas like mountaintops or coastal headlands, the whole plant community is influenced by the prevailing winds. Plants may be low and stunted, all leaning in the direction the wind constantly pushes them.
- Wind is also crucial to plants that rely on it to spread their pollen or seed: without wind they would not be able to produce future generations of their species.

◆ *Tie streamers to a tree to gauge wind direction and speed.* ◆

Flowerpots

Make a flowerpot for yourself or as a gift for a friend. Painted green and decorated with plaid ribbons, it makes for a great Christmas gift: ideal for a teacher's (holiday) present, or for a grandparent interested in gardening. It can also be painted in other colors, to match with any indoor setting.

- ◆ nontoxic spray paint
- ◆ decorations of your choice: ribbons, dried flowers, seed pods
- ◆ plants to pot

WHAT TO DO

Cut the ridge off the top of the margarine container and make several small holes in the bottom to allow for drainage.

Glue on the popsicle sticks one at a time around the sides of the container, being careful to space them evenly. You will need to leave little gaps between the sticks at the top so that they will be straight. Allow ample time for the glue to dry before painting.

Spray paint the pot in a color of your choice.

Decorate with ribbons, sprigs of dried flowers, or seed pods.

Choose a plant to place in your pot (see next page, Pretty Plants for Indoor Pots). Select one that is growing in a container only a little bit smaller than your popsicle pot. When you transfer the plant, the roots will then have some room to grow.

Transfer your plant from its old pot to your popsicle pot (see next page, Potting a Plant, What to Do).

Find a light, airy spot to place your pot and it will live for many weeks indoors.

Flowerpot

A flowerpot is easy to put together and looks terrific filled with flowering annuals.

YOU WILL NEED

- ◆ a margarine container
- ◆ safety scissors
- ◆ craft glue
- ◆ popsicle sticks

Pretty Plants for Indoor Pots

Many annuals can be grown from seedlings or even grown from seed and will live for several weeks indoors. Plants of English daisy, fairy primrose, polyanthus, scarlet sage, or pot marigold are suitable for an indoor flowerpot. If you wish to start your plant from seed, use nasturtium: the seeds are large and germinate easily. "Alaska" would be a suitable nasturtium cultivar to choose as it grows into a neat plant unlike most cultivars which have long floppy stems. "Alaska" has pretty green and white (variegated) leaves and bright flowers.

Potting a Plant

YOU WILL NEED

- a container with holes at the bottom for drainage
- potting mix
- a plant that has outgrown its pot
- water

WHAT TO DO

Place some potting mix in the bottom of your container.

Turn the plant out of its old container. Be careful not to disturb the roots too much.

Place the root ball in the new pot, centering the plant.

Fill around the root ball with potting mix and firm down with your fingers.

Leave a space of ½ inch (1 cm) at the top of the container to enable you to water the plant.

Water well and allow to drain before taking the plant inside.

Caring for Your Plant

YOU WILL NEED

- a potted plant
- water
- slow-release fertilizer
- a well-lit, well-ventilated spot

WHAT TO DO

Sprinkle a teaspoonful of slow-release fertilizer granules around the potting mix to ensure healthy growth.

Place your plant in a well-lit, well-ventilated spot indoors.

Water your plant outside when the top 1¼ inch (3 cm) of potting mix feels dry.

Turn the pot plant around now and then, especially if it is near a window, so that growth will be even—plants grow toward the light.

Cut off any dying flowers so that new ones will grow in their place.

Wipe the leaves gently with a damp cloth if they get dusty.

Note: When the plant begins to get a bit tired and ragged looking, plant it out in the garden.

GARDENING TIP

TRANSPLANTING

Only transfer a plant into a container one size larger. Putting a tiny plant into a big pot causes the roots to remain wet, and the plant will suffer.

When you are planting in a pot, choose a plant with a root system only a little smaller than your container.

If you are growing from seed, you'll need to transplant several times, into a bigger container each time, until it reaches the right size for your pot.

♦ *Watering and fertilizing help plants to grow.* ♦

92

Lots of Pots!

There are many different types of pots and hanging baskets that you can buy to grow plants in. Pots come in several shapes and sizes and are made from plastic, clay, cement, or ceramics. Hanging baskets are made from either plastic or wire with some type of natural fiber. There are also lots of containers that you might find around the house to use as pots for your plants. You might find:

- an old tin bucket
- a plastic bucket
- chipped mugs or cups that are no longer used
- an old ceramic pitcher
- cereal bowls
- glass jars (paint them first—roots don't like light)
- an old china or metal teapot
- an old wheelbarrow
- a wooden box (line it with plastic and cut a few holes before you plant)
- a cane basket (lined with plastic, like the wooden box)
- plastic ice-cream containers (decorated with paint)
- a hollowed-out log

PLANTS CAN MOVE!

You might think plants can't move because it is natural to think of movement that is noticeable, for instance, people getting up and walking around. Plants can move but their movements are fairly slow and are, therefore, hard to see. They are also set off by forces outside the plant itself.

A good way to test plant movement is with indoor plants. Light stimulates a plant to grow toward it. Put your indoor plants in a room next to a window. Does your plant grow toward the light? You will find that the growing tips of plants move or bend toward the light source.

If you have sunflowers growing, you will notice they follow the light too. They are like solar trackers as they hold their leaves and flowers out, following the sun's path during the day.

Other types of plant movement are flowers closing at night and opening again in the morning. Dandelions and tulips do this.

Have you ever seen an insect-eating plant like the Venus Flytrap? It snaps shut to trap and eat any small insect that comes too close.

The leaves of mimosa quickly snap shut like a fan and droop when touched. When you go away, they open up and return to normal. No prizes for guessing its common name: Sensitive Plant or Touch-me-not!

Potted plants need good drainage. They will die if any excess water remains to rot their roots. All containers must have a drainage hole to allow the water to run off. If you can't make a hole in the bottom of a container, you can put a "pot within a pot." This means that you can use a normal plastic pot to hold your plant and then put it inside the other, prettier pot without the hole. Take the plastic pot out to water the plant and put it back in when all water has drained away.

Sowing Seed

Growing plants from seed is an inexpensive way to create a garden. Annuals and vegetables are raised from seeds. Check the seed packets at your local garden store to find many different annuals and vegetables to sow!

How to Sow Seeds

YOU WILL NEED

- a clean pot or waterproof container
- potting mix
- a tamper (a small piece of wood to press down the potting mix)
- water and a hose
- seeds
- a popsicle stick
- a plastic bag
- a twist tie
- a pen

WHAT TO DO

Add the mix to the pot or container until it is three-quarters filled.

Firm down well using the tamper. The mix should be lightly compacted.

Water the mix using a hose turned to a fine mist spray.

Spread the seeds on the mix, making sure not to overcrowd them.

- For large seeds, place a few by hand, spacing them well.
- For medium-size seeds, broadcast by hand.
- For very small seeds, combine with sand and sprinkle over the mix, for even spacing.

> ### GARDENING TIP
>
> #### RAISING SEEDS IN POTS
> - Squat, rectangular-shaped pots are ideal for raising plants from seed.
> - Always use a potting mix when planting seeds. It has the right amount of sand and peat in it to keep the seeds moist enough to germinate without being soggy. It is available in bags at nurseries and supermarkets.

Cover the seeds with a little of the mix. Don't cover too deeply. If the seeds are very fine, don't cover at all. A good rule for most seeds other than fine ones, is to make the depth of the covering twice that of the diameter of the seed. Seeds will have difficulty growing if they are planted too deep.

◆◆◆

A sealed plastic bag creates a warm, moist environment.

◆◆◆

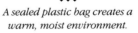

◆ *Sowing seeds in containers.* ◆

Press gently with the tamper. There should be ½ inch (1 cm) between the top of the mix and the top of the container, so that the seeds will not run out of the pot when watered.

Water gently again with the fine mist spray of the hose.

Write the type of seed you are sowing and the date on the popsicle stick, just in case you forget what it is later.

Push the popsicle stick down into the side of the pot.

Place the container in a plastic bag and seal with a twist tie.

Keep in a warm spot.

DID YOU KNOW?

You don't need to rush out to the shop to buy seed for your gardening activities when you have so many already in the kitchen at home! You can save and use seeds of avocados, lemons, oranges, passion fruit, cantaloupe, watermelons (suitable for warm climates only), as well as tomatoes, cucumbers, peas, beans, sweet peppers, pumpkins, apples, pears, and peaches.

Growing Sweet Peas

In many parts of the world, sweet peas are traditionally planted on St. Patrick's Day, March 17. It is fun to remember the patron saint of Ireland by planting the seeds on this day. They can, however, be planted any time in autumn or early spring in places that have a very cold winter. If you live in a temperate climate, sow seed from mid-summer to late autumn. Autumn is the time to plant if you live in a hot climate with little or no winter.

Sweet peas are a sweetly scented annual. The seeds will germinate, grow into a climbing vine, flower, produce seed, and die all within the space of one year. They are easy to grow and the flowers are delightful to pick for a bouquet.

♦♦♦

Growing Sweet Peas

YOU WILL NEED

- a support for the plant: wooden lattice, wire mesh, or a tripod
- complete fertilizer
- garden lime
- a packet of sweet pea seeds
- water

WHAT TO DO

Choose a sunny position, sheltered from strong winds: against a fence is ideal as it is easier to erect the support by nailing on the chicken wire or lattice. Ask an adult to help you choose a spot and make the support. Sweet peas like well-drained soil so don't plant them where it is always damp.

Add complete fertilizer and 1 cup of lime to each square yard of soil. Dig over and rake flat. Leave for 1 week before planting.

Make holes in the ground ¾ inch (2 cm) deep and at intervals of 4 inches (10 cm) in front of the trellis or support.

Place 1 seed in each hole, cover with soil and firm down.

Water until the soil is moist but not soggy.

Watch your plants grow. In 2 weeks, the seedlings will have grown up through the soil. It will take the plants 3–4 months to flower.

GARDENING TIP

For faster germination of sweet pea seeds, place the seeds on wet paper overnight and then plant them the next day in their final location.

DID YOU KNOW?

Sweet pea seeds that are small and look shriveled are usually the ones that produce dark-colored flowers. Plant some and see if this is true.

Sweet Peas in Pots

There are some types of sweet pea plants that don't climb but are bushy in habit. These suit pots and you don't have to make a support for them as you would with climbing sweet peas. Try "Bijou," or "Cupid," or "Little Sweethearts."

Plant dwarf types of sweet peas in pots.

WIN

T Ě R

Garden Discovery in Winter

In some places, winter barely makes its mark and gardening tasks can continue. In colder areas, use winter as a time to think about and plan for the gardening year ahead. Draw up plans for next season's annual plot or potting activities or make lists of tasks and things to plant. Go out and gather cones, twigs, and pods for craft. You may find ripe pods, capsules, nuts, or berries that have seeds inside. Collect and store the seeds for planting in spring. Indoor gardening and garden craft activities are ideal for days that are too unpleasant for venturing outside.

❖❖❖

Even though the pace of gardening slows down in winter, there are still many interesting things to find and tasks to do.

❖❖❖

Rainy Day Blues

Spend dismal rainy days doing indoor gardening activities. There are many to choose from. Try some of the following ideas!

Colored Celery

YOU WILL NEED

- a celery stalk
- water
- a glass jar
- food coloring

WHAT TO DO

Pour water into the jar until it is half full.
Add several drops of red or blue food coloring.
Place the celery stalk in the jar.
Wait for a few hours.
What has happened?

Plants need water to survive. It is easier to see how they take up moisture when the water is colored with food coloring.

Begin a Bean Stalk

Bean seeds germinate readily. You can buy seed packets of string beans (the ones you most commonly eat) at nurseries, or try the supermarket. Supermarkets carry a range of dried bean seeds for cooking. They are quite inexpensive and work equally well. Select from broad beans, red kidney beans, black-eyed beans, soybeans, or lima beans.

YOU WILL NEED

- bean seeds
- a glass jar
- water

WHAT TO DO

Add some bean seeds to the glass jar.
Add plenty of water so that the beans are fully submerged.
Soak the beans in water for 2–3 days to soften their outer coat. This will trigger germination and the beans will send out a long shoot.
Drain off the water.
Keep the bean seedlings moist in the jar and let them continue growing until their leaves appear.
Plant the bean shoots outside and you may grow a very tall bean stalk that produces a crop of beans!

Grow a Salad

Alfalfa seeds are quick to sprout and useful for adding to salads once they have produced soft green shoots. You need only a small amount of seeds to grow a jar full of delicious and nutritious alfalfa sprouts.

◆ *1 tablespoon of seeds produces a glassful of shoots.* ◆

YOU WILL NEED

- alfalfa seeds (other seeds to sprout are mustard and cress)
- a glass jar
- warm water
- an old stocking
- an elastic band

WHAT TO DO

Place 1 tablespoonful of alfalfa seeds in a clean glass jar.

Cover with warm water and allow the seeds to soak for 3 minutes.

Place a clean piece of the old stocking over the top of the jar and secure it with the elastic band.

Tip the jar on its side so that all the water runs off into the sink.

Repeat the rinsing and draining treatment twice a day, morning and night. Watch your sprouts grow a little each day. Within several days, your alfalfa sprouts will be ready to eat.

Root Vegetable Leafy Tops

Root vegetables—carrots, radishes, parsnips, turnips, beets—will grow leafy tops if given a little moisture.

YOU WILL NEED

- the tops of any root vegetable
- gravel
- a glass jar
- water

WHAT TO DO

Add gravel to the glass jar until it is three-quarters filled.

Add a little water.

Place the cutoff tops of the vegetables on top of the gravel.

Watch what happens over time. Leaves will regrow from the vegetable tops, but the root, the underground part that you eat, will not.

◆◆◆
Any root vegetables can be used for the Vegetable Tops experiment. Here, radish tops are growing.
◆◆◆

Become a Mushroom Farmer

Mushroom kits can be purchased from specialty catalogs. They come with all the necessary materials and full instructions. You might like to have a small one of your own. If your family has a kit, transfer a little of the materials to your own box lined with plastic. Remember, mushrooms like moisture and limited light so you will need to provide them with these requirements in order for them to thrive.

Mushrooms are plants even though they do not have green leaves or produce flowers. They do not need sunlight to grow because they do not produce chlorophyll. Also, they reproduce by way of spores rather than by seeds. Spores are tiny and hard to see. Pick one of your mature mushrooms, take off the stem, and leave the cap on a sheet of white paper for a day or so. The spores will fall out and leave a print on the paper.

♦ *Preparing homegrown mushrooms for dinner.* ♦

YOU WILL NEED

- a mushroom kit
- a wooden or cardboard box
- plastic lining
- water
- a spray bottle

WHAT TO DO

Line your box with plastic.

Transfer some of the mushroom compost from the kit into your box.

Follow the instructions on the kit for adding the mushroom spore and watering.

Water your mushrooms when necessary, using the mist setting on the spray bottle.

DANGER !

Some mushrooms and other fungi are poisonous. If you see any growing in the garden, do not touch or eat them.

Make a Terrarium

YOU WILL NEED

- a large glass container with a wide neck and lid
- gravel or small stones
- potting mix, a small amount
- plants: small ferns, tiny African violets, or cyclamen are good choices
- a mister and water

WHAT TO DO

Line the bottom of the jar with gravel or small stones and add some potting mix to the bottom of the container.

Arrange plants carefully in the terrarium.

Water with a mister, being careful not to add too much moisture because the plants will rot in damp conditions.

Place the lid on the jar. Alternate with the lid on and off, removing it when the sides of the glass get misty.

◆ *Plants growing in a terrarium need to be watered only lightly.* ◆

Bringing in Birds

The best way to attract birds to your garden is to provide a suitable habitat for them. Make your outdoor space similar to their natural home. Plant thickets of tall trees, shrubby bushes, and grasses. Dense shrubs are used by small birds to rest and nest.

Plants with berries, flowers, nectar, or seed that birds like to eat can be introduced as a food source. Provide water in a shallow pond or birdbath. If you have a cat as a pet, make sure that it has a bell on its collar to give the birds warning that a predator is around!

Feeding birds will attract them to your garden, but once you start, make sure you continue because the birds will begin to rely on you for their food. Don't feed birds honey or sugar mixtures; seed in a bird feeder or on a tray will do the trick and is much healthier for them.

You can buy seed bells at supermarkets or pet shops to hang in trees. It is great fun watching birds eating off these bells, especially when they hang upside down to eat and do other funny tricks.

Make a Simple Bird Feeder

YOU WILL NEED

- a saucer-shaped clay pot or plastic bowl
- bird seed
- 3 pieces of rope, each 3 feet (1 m) long
- a wire hoop

WHAT TO DO

Fill the pot or bowl with seed. If you are using a pot, cover any drainage hole before adding the seed.

Knot the 3 pieces of rope together in the middle.

Tie the 6 ends of rope together and insert a wire hoop.

Place the pot or bowl in the bottom of the rope loop and hang up in a tree.

♦♦♦
Fill feeders with bird seed.
♦♦♦

Five Little Dickeybirds

The Grevillea bush, a common plant in some areas, has bird-shaped seed pods, ideal for a craft activity. If Grevillea bushes are common to your area, gather some seed pods and make 5 little dickeybirds!

YOU WILL NEED

- 5 seed pods from a Grevillea bush
- cotton balls
- craft glue
- 10 plastic eyes

WHAT TO DO

Pinch off a small amount of the pink cotton balls.

Roll it into a small ball.

Place a little glue into the open seed pod and push in the cotton ball.

Glue a small plastic eye onto each side of the bird's face.

Make 4 more birds the same way.

Balls, Bubbles, and Balloons

⊥ Cool but clear winter days are an ideal time to dress warmly and venture outside for some warming-up activites and games. There are many things to do using balls and balloons, with friends or on your own. You can also try some bubble blowing and make your own solution and wand.

Balls

Balls of all shapes, sizes, and weights are fun to play with outside. Begin with simple throwing and catching exercises. Place an old garbage can on the lawn, stand away from it and throw your ball into it. Try again, but this time run in the general space and throw while running. Stand on the spot, throwing the ball up into the air and catching it. Throw it higher and higher each time. You could also try bouncing it on a hard surface or throwing it at a target on a wall and catching it when it bounces off. If you have a friend to play with, try throwing overarm and underarm to each other. The smaller the ball, the harder these tasks will be. Begin by using a large ball, then move on to a smaller ball. When you're really skilled, try using a tennis ball. Once you have mastered these tasks, you could find a section of lawn or a paved or concreted area and have fun playing some of the following games.

Skittles

Collect 6 empty plastic soft drink bottles.
Fill them with water, and add a few drops of food coloring. The water makes them stand more securely and the color makes them attractive.
Place the bottles in a triangle, pointed toward the player.
Give each player 3 balls to bowl at them. A heavy ball, such as a soccer ball, would work best.
To score: Allow 1 point for each bottle knocked down. Award 3 extra points if all the skittles are knocked down on the first bowl!

Monkey in the Middle

Choose 2 players to throw a ball back and forth to each other, while keeping on the run.
Choose a third player (the monkey) to be in the middle.
Throw the ball back and forth until the monkey catches it. The monkey will change places with the last player to throw the ball.

Strike one!

♦ *Floating away on the breeze.* ♦

Bubbles

Bubble blowing is an easy activity to prepare and will give you hours of fun!

YOU WILL NEED

- ¼ cup (60 ml) liquid detergent
- a few drops glycerine
- ½ cup (125 ml) water
- a cup
- a bubble wand: a piece of wire or a pipe cleaner about 8 inches (20 cm) long, bent and twisted at about 3 inches (8 cm) from the end. Open out the end to form a complete circle.

WHAT TO DO

Place the detergent, glycerine, and water in the cup and stir gently.

Dip the circular part of your bubble wand completely into the mixture, take it out, and blow.

Use big balloons to play punching ball.

Bubble Blowing Games

Once you have made your own bubble solution and wand, try some of the following games. Why not invite some of your friends to join in the fun?

- Blow slowly to make a huge bubble.
- Blow quickly to make many small bubbles.
- Blow a bubble and try to catch it back again on your wand.
- If you're playing with a friend, blow a bubble to your partner who has to try to catch it (make sure you don't blow the detergent into your friend's eyes).

Balloons

Balloons come in all different colors, shapes, and sizes: from tiny water balloons to giant ones that need lots of big breaths to blow up. They can be round or oval as well as shaped like a long sausage.

Balloons are much easier than balls to throw and catch, because they move at a slower pace. Begin learning your ball skills with a balloon before you move on to a ball. There are many other ways to play with a balloon, too.

Balloon Games

- Blow up a balloon but do not make a knot at the neck; let it go and watch it fly.
- Tie some balloons with string and hang them in trees to bat with your hands.
- Tie a balloon onto a string; hold the string and play punching ball with your fist.
- For a party game, run while holding a balloon between your knees.

Roots and Shoots

↥ A bulb's green shoots poking up out of the earth in spring awakens us to the thrill and excitement of a new season. When flowering, bulbs are one of the prettiest additions to a garden. However, to really see how a bulb grows, the best method is to raise one in water in a vase. You will be able to watch the bulb grow, observing what normally happens beneath the soil.

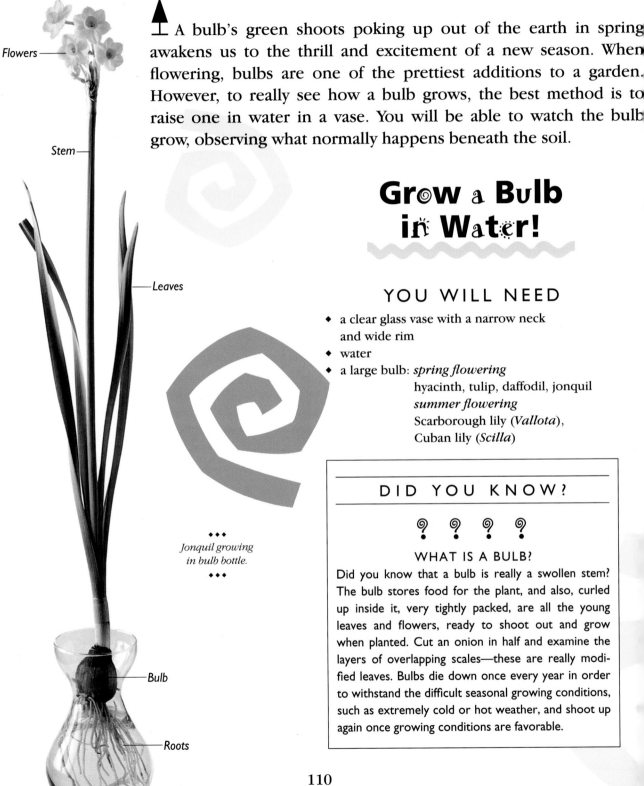

Flowers

Stem

Leaves

•••
*Jonquil growing
in bulb bottle.*
•••

Bulb

Roots

Grow a Bulb in Water!

YOU WILL NEED

- a clear glass vase with a narrow neck and wide rim
- water
- a large bulb: *spring flowering*
  hyacinth, tulip, daffodil, jonquil
  summer flowering
  Scarborough lily (*Vallota*),
  Cuban lily (*Scilla*)

DID YOU KNOW?

WHAT IS A BULB?

Did you know that a bulb is really a swollen stem? The bulb stores food for the plant, and also, curled up inside it, very tightly packed, are all the young leaves and flowers, ready to shoot out and grow when planted. Cut an onion in half and examine the layers of overlapping scales—these are really modified leaves. Bulbs die down once every year in order to withstand the difficult seasonal growing conditions, such as extremely cold or hot weather, and shoot up again once growing conditions are favorable.

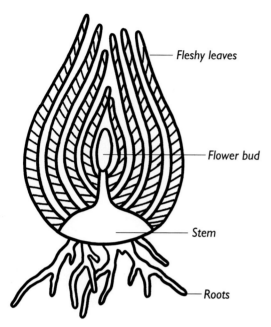

Fleshy leaves

Flower bud

Stem

Roots

◆ *Young leaves and flower in a bulb.* ◆

WHAT TO DO

Fill the glass vase with water up to its neck.

Place the bulb in the top of the vase so it sits comfortably in the neck. It must not slip down too far. Make sure the water is just touching the bottom of the bulb.

Put the vase in a cool, dark place until the roots are well developed.

Bring the vase into a brightly lit room and the bulb will send up green leaves (shoots). In time, it will flower.

Onion Experiment

For this experiment, you can use any type of bulb. Ornamental bulbs are usually grown, but sometimes it is more convenient to use a bulb from the kitchen. On a miserable, wet day, it is easier to grab an onion bulb or a garlic clove from the kitchen than it is to dig up a daffodil or tulip bulb from the garden.

YOU WILL NEED

- ◆ a plant bulb
- ◆ toothpicks
- ◆ a glass jar
- ◆ water

WHAT TO DO

Insert toothpicks around the bulb of your choice so it will sit securely on the rim of the glass jar.

Add water to the jar until the top of the liquid just reaches the bottom of the bulb.

Watch what happens over time: the roots will grow, followed by the shoots. If you are really interested, you could nurture your plant in its jar until it flowers.

◆ ◆ ◆
An onion will send out roots and shoots just like any other bulb.
◆ ◆ ◆

Hairy Harry

⬆ You can make a Hairy Harry eggshell person with growing hair at any time of the year. However, it is most rewarding in winter when it may be too cold to go outside to grow things in the garden.

Eggshell Person

YOU WILL NEED

- an eggcup
- a red felt pen
- craft glue
- water
- seeds (see Seeds to Use below)
- an empty eggshell
- plastic eyes
- a cotton ball

CRAFT TIP

🎨 🎨 🎨 🎨

SEEDS TO USE
- cress seed to make Charlie Cress
- mustard seed for Mustard Mary
- wheat seed for Wally Wheat
- grass seed for Gertrude Grass

YOU COULD ALSO USE
- a potato with the top scooped out and sprinkled with seed to grow hair. Add other vegetables held on with toothpicks for the facial features.
- a coconut shell filled with potting mix and grass seed for hair.
- the foot of an old stocking filled with potting mix. Place grass seed in the stocking, add the potting mix, and tie up the stocking. Water and, in a week or so, the hair will grow up out of the stocking!

WHAT TO DO

Place the empty eggshell in the eggcup, with the broken end up.

Draw a mouth with the red felt pen.

Glue on the eyes and allow to dry.

Place the cotton ball inside the shell.

Sprinkle on a little seed.

Water sparingly. In about 3 days the seed will germinate, and within a week your person will have a lush head of hair!

◆◆◆

*Hairy Harry growing
green hair!*

◆◆◆

Beautiful Bark

You would be surprised at how many different types of bark there are on trees. Some trees have smooth trunks, whereas others have rough ones. Sometimes bark has a powdery coating over it, whereas other bark may be shiny. Trees can have bark that peels off in strips or falls off in chunks or plates. Bark can have horizontal or vertical ridges, large holes, or small indentations. You can find quite a number of different bark types on the trees just in your own backyard. Go out and discover how many you can find. It is much easier to see the differences in bark and compare the patterns if you take a bark rubbing.

Bark Rubbing

YOU WILL NEED

- a tree
- a piece of paper
- adhesive tape
- a thick crayon

WHAT TO DO

Tape the paper onto the tree trunk.
Rub firmly, using the side of the crayon, over the paper. The pattern of the bark will be transferred onto the paper.

What Is Bark?

Bark surrounds a woody plant's trunk and branches. The outer layer is thick and corky and protects the plant; the inner layer of bark contains the vessels that transport food throughout the plant. Bark not only is an attractive feature, but also plays a major role in the survival of a tree. Be careful not to damage the bark, and do not move a complete ring of bark from the tree trunk. If you do, the tree's food supply may be cut off and the tree may die or be seriously harmed as a result.

DID YOU KNOW?

THE USES OF BARK

- Cinnamon is a spice used to flavor foods. It comes from the inner bark of the cinnamon tree. The bark is wet, then stripped, cleaned, and left to dry. It curls up tightly in rolls while drying.
- Cork comes from the bark of cork oak trees. Once it is stripped away from the trees, it grows back. Cork is used as a bottle stopper and is also an excellent floor covering and soundproofing material.
- Tanbark is bark that has been put through a tanning process. It is then broken up into small chips and used as a ground cover in playgrounds and landscaped gardens.

◆ *Bark rubbing highlights the texture of a tree's bark.* ◆

Seed Pod Sculpture

Gather together all the wonderful nature objects and plant bits and pieces you've found in the garden and have saved throughout the year. Craft them into people, animals, or anything else you'd like—be imaginative! Make your sculpture realistic and lifelike or as strange and fanciful as you wish.

◆ *Pine cone family at the beach.* ◆

Seed Pod Sculpture

YOU WILL NEED

- a variety of dried seed pods: pine cones, acorns, eucalyptus seed capsules, honesty, liquidambar, and plane tree pods
- other objects from the garden such as twigs, stones, snail shells, and feathers
- large seeds, such as avocado
- quick-drying glue
- paint, craft eyes, or yarn for hair (optional)

WHAT TO DO

Arrange your seed pods and other nature objects to create a piece of sculpture. **Glue** the pieces together. **Decorate** with paint, craft eyes, or yarn, if you wish.

◆◆◆
Seed pod sculptures are easy-to-make, long-lasting decorations.
◆◆◆

CRAFT TIP

A hot-glue gun can be used to make sure that all the parts of your sculpture stay together. Always ask an adult to do the gluing for you because the gun and glue can get very hot. Hot-glue guns and glue sticks are available at fabric stores.

If the bottom of your sculpture is rough and likely to scratch the furniture, glue a piece of felt underneath it.

If you would like your sculpture to have a glossy finish, spray or paint it with a clear varnish. Always varnish in a well-ventilated area.

DID YOU KNOW?

Pine cones grow on trees called conifers. Conifers hold their seeds in cones rather than in fruit. Forests full of conifer trees cover a large part of the Earth's surface. Conifers include some of the tallest, oldest, and most massive trees in the world.

Plant a Tree— Save the Earth

Earth Day is celebrated on April 22. A good way to celebrate this special day is by planting a tree to help the environment. All plants take in carbon dioxide and give out oxygen, so the more trees we plant, the better the air we breathe. Help make air—plant a tree!

How to Choose Trees

* Make a list of trees you like: look through plant books or gardening magazines. You might include ones with beautiful flowers, a handsome shape, or those with rich autumn leaf color.
* Consider the area in which you live. Are the trees on your list going to grow well in your suburb? Go for a walk around your neighborhood. Mark off any of the trees on your list that you can see are healthy and growing well.
* Take your list to a local nursery and ask the staff to help you. Tell them how high you want your tree to grow and where you are going to plant it (sun, shade, close to the house, away from the house). Show your list and they will be able to help you choose which tree is best for you from those you have marked.

How to Plant a Tree

Once you have made your choice, purchased a tree, and brought it home, there are several things to do to get it off to a good start in your garden.

YOU WILL NEED

* a suitable spot in the garden
* compost or organic matter
* a young tree from the plant nursery
* water

WHAT TO DO

Prepare the planting area by digging and loosening the topsoil, and adding compost or organic matter (see Winter, A Worm Farm, page 122).

Dig a square hole as deep and twice as wide as the pot holding your plant.

Water the plant in its pot until it is well soaked.

Tap the plant out of its pot and position it in the hole. Make sure the top of the potting mix is level with the ground because it shouldn't be planted any deeper.

Backfill with the soil you dug from the hole and gently press down with your hands.

Mulch with leaf litter or compost; water well and regularly until your tree is established.

◆ Planting a magnolia tree. ◆

Planting Trees for Special Occasions

Planting trees need not be confined to one day of the year. Occasions can be made more special and memorable by planting a tree. As the years go by and the tree grows taller and stronger, it is nice to think back and remember the reason it was planted, who planted it, or for whom it was planted. You might like to plant a tree to honor:

♦ the birth of a new family member
♦ your birthday
♦ the death of a pet
♦ when you started school
♦ when someone in your family gets married

Botanical Names

Botanists use very long Latin names to classify plants. They are difficult to remember, so most people call plants by special names that are easier to understand—common names. Look at the list of climbing trees on the following page and you will see the common name first and the botanical name after it. Which is easier to remember?

Throughout this book, common names are used. Sometimes common names change from region to region or from one country to another. Botanical names, however, are always the same throughout the world. For this reason, they can be useful and sometimes are absolutely necessary to use so that the exact plant being referred to is clear to all readers.

♦♦♦
Climbing trees are geat to climb, swing off, or just hang around in!
♦♦♦

Climbing Trees

If you have a big tree in your garden to climb, swing off, or make a tree house in, you are very lucky indeed. If you don't have one, a parent might be interested in planting a climbing tree. It should be big and strong: climbing trees are heavy-duty trees with sturdy trunks and branches. Those with brittle wood are not suitable. It should also have limbs reasonably close to the ground for you to get a foothold. Make sure your garden is large enough to support such a tree. It is also crucial to position it sensibly. Make sure the species you select is suited to your region and climate. Avoid species that have sharp thorns on their trunk or branches and steer clear of any tree with poisonous leaves, fruit, or sap.

SOME SUGGESTIONS

Beech	*Fagus sylvatica*
Black bean	*Castanospermum australe*
Box elder maple	*Acer negundo*
Brush box	*Lophostemon confertus*
Chinese elm	*Ulmus parvifolia*
Golden elm	*Ulmus glabra* 'Lutescens'
Jacaranda	*Jacaranda mimosifolia*
Liquidambar	*Liquidambar styraciflua*
Oak	*Quercus robur*
Pepper tree	*Schinus areira*
Plane tree	*Platanus* spp.
Poinciana	*Delonix regia*
Tulip tree	*Liriodendron tulipifera*

◆◆◆
Trees come in different shapes.
◆◆◆

domed   vase shaped

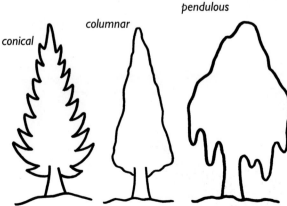

conical   columnar   pendulous

A Worm Farm

Worms live in water, soil, and decaying material from plants and animals. They are found all over the world except in dry or arid areas and arctic regions. They are very important helpers in mixing the soil and bringing air into it. They also play a vital part in providing food for plants. Gardeners value worms very much and in your vegetable or flower garden, you can encourage earthworm populations. Make a worm farm, increase the number of worms you have, and then return them to the garden.

◆ *These boys are having a wonderful time getting their worms ready for the worm farm.* ◆

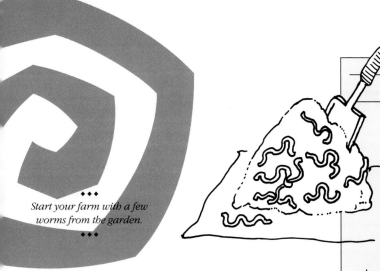

Start your farm with a few worms from the garden.

WONDERFUL WORMS

Worms are good for your garden. Did you know earthworms break down soil and organic matter by eating it, working it through their bodies, and passing it out as nutrient-rich wormcasts or manure? While they burrow down through the earth, they also make small tunnels that allow air (oxygen) to get to the plant roots. These tunnels also enable water to filter down to the roots during periods of rain and moisture to drain away quickly so the soil does not become soggy.

Make a Worm Farm

YOU WILL NEED

♦ a glass jar
♦ soil
♦ organic matter: decayed leaves, twigs, flowers, or fruit of garden plants
♦ water
♦ worms

WHAT TO DO

Add soil and organic matter from the garden to the glass jar until it is half full.

Water the mixture lightly and keep it moist.

Dig some worms from the garden. If you live in an apartment, you can buy worms from a fish bait store.

Place the worms in the soil.

Watch your worms. What do they eat? Are they always moving? How do they grow? To keep your worms happy, make sure they have enough moisture. Give them organic matter, like decaying leaves, for food. They also like to be kept fairly cool.

In time, your worms will multiply. Place some back in the garden when you have a large number as they will help in soil building. You can also add them to your compost bin, where they will break down kitchen scraps and garden refuse into rich compost.

OTHER FARMS TO MAKE

♦ ant colony (make sure you collect a queen as well as workers)
♦ silkworm farm
♦ pillbug place
♦ snail city
♦ caterpillar cottage
♦ ladybird lair

To make any of these colonies, provide each type of insect, beetle, or bug with the conditions they prefer. Give them food and water. Observe them and then let them go.

Make a Home for Your Worms: A Compost Bin

A compost bin is a great home for your worms. Very effective bins can be bought from nurseries, and you can make compost by adding a variety of materials to them. A large plastic bin with the bottom cut out is cheaper and works just as well.

Add kitchen scraps and autumn leaves to your compost bin. They will rot down to become humus.

◆◆◆

YOU WILL NEED

- a large plastic bin with a lid
- compost materials, chopped up finely (see below)
- worms
- water

COMPOST MATERIALS

- vegetable peels and scraps
- fruit peels and scraps
- used tea bags
- eggshells
- egg cartons
- animal manure: horse, cow, or chicken
- autumn leaves
- plant prunings
- lawn clippings

MATERIALS TO AVOID

- diseased plants
- weeds that grow from a bulb—if any weeds you pull up have a swelling like a tiny onion above the roots, don't add them to your bin
- meat scraps
- fatty scraps
- bones

WHAT TO DO

Place the bin in a sunny position as the sun will heat up everything inside, breaking down your leaves and vegetable scraps quicker.

Place the compost materials in the bin.

Add the worms.

Water gently and keep moist but not wet while your compost is decomposing. Put the lid on after watering.

Add new materials as you get them, until the bin is full.

Wait. After several months, you will have a rich compost, ready to add to your garden plot.

Wear gardening gloves when handling compost or when moving it from your bin for use in the garden.

Useful Box

The garden provides a wonderful array of bits and pieces that can be collected and used for craft activities.

Be on the lookout for:

- feathers
- interesting bark
- twigs
- seed pods
- conifer cones
- eucalyptus seed capsules

- autumn leaves
- smooth stones
- grass seed
- large seeds, such as avocado
- snail shells
- flowers for drying or pressing

◆ *Keep craft materials in a box so they will stay in good condition, clean and dust-free.* ◆

Glossary

- **annual** A plant that lives for only 1 year. During that time a seed will germinate, grow into a plant, flower, produce seed, and then die.

- **bark** A thick, corky layer surrounding and protecting the trunk and branches of some plants.

- **broadcast** To take a handful of seeds or fertilizer and throw it on the ground. This will scatter the seeds or fertilizer evenly.

- **bud** A small, baby shoot on a plant. It holds the new leaves or flowers, all packed tightly in a bundle.

- **bulb** A swollen stem that is planted underground. Roots grow from its base and leaves shoot up through the ground into the air. An onion is a bulb.

- **bush/dwarf variety** A variety of plant that is smaller and neater in habit than the usual type.

- **chlorophyll** The green coloring of leaves and plants.

- **compost** A mixture of organic residues that may include rotted-down plant materials, manure, and eggshells. Add to your garden and it will nourish the soil and plants.

- **cultivar** A plant or vegetable that differs a little from its species and that has been cultivated for these special characteristics. Botanists give very long Latin names to all plants. For instance all carrots are called *Daucus carota*. Some special cultivars of carrots are: *Daucus carota* "All Seasons," with a large tapering root to 8 inches (20 cm); *Daucus carota* "Topweight," having a medium-colored orange root with a pale core, the roots grow to about 7 inches (18 cm); *Daucus carota* "Tom Thumb" is still a carrot but it has small, round, orange roots.

- **deadheading** To cut the dead or dying flowers off a plant.

- **deciduous** A plant that sheds leaves in winter.

- **dig over** To dig into the soil with a spade or fork to a depth of about 8 inches (20 cm) and turn it over so the bottom layer comes to the top and the top layer is mixed with the bottom.

- **direct sowing** To place seed straight into the position you wish to grow the plant in the garden bed.

- **dormant** Not growing, but still alive.

- **earthworm** A worm that burrows and digs in the soil. It feeds on the soil and decaying organic matter.

- **fallow** Let the soil lie for a time without doing anything to it.

- **fertilize** When pollen from a male flower (or male flower part) reaches the ovary of the female flower part.

- **fertilizer** A combination of all the chemical elements that plants need for life (other than oxygen, carbon, and hydrogen, which they get from air and water).
  - **slow-release fertilizer** Small balls of fertilizer that gradually dissolve in the soil, releasing the food slowly.
  - **liquid fertilizer** Powdered fertilizer

that dissolves when added to water or a concentrated liquid fertilizer that needs to be diluted in water. It is applied with a watering can.
– complete fertilizer Some fertilizers have only 1 or 2 of the foods a plant needs to grow. A complete fertilizer has all 13 of them.

• **fruit** The part of a plant that develops from a flower and bears the seed.

• **germinate** When the hard outer coating of a seed softens and the root and shoot begin to grow out of the seed.

• **glut** Too much of one vegetable or fruit to eat at once.

• **habit** The shape a plant grows into, e.g., tall, bushy, ground cover.

• **harvest** To pick fruit and vegetables off the plant.

• **herb** Soft-stemmed, bushy plants valued for their smell and taste; often used in cooking or perfumery.

• **inorganic** Coming from a nonliving thing, e.g., chemical, man-made.

• **life cycle** The life of a living thing, plant or animal: beginning, going through all stages, reproducing, and then ending.

• **manure** The droppings of animals. Horse, cow, chicken, or rabbit manure is great compost for gardens.

• **monoecious** Male and female flowers on the one plant.

• **organic** Anything that was once living.

• **ovary** One of the female parts of a

flower. After fertilization, it swells and becomes the fruit.

• **ovule** Lies within the ovary and contains the egg cell. After fertilization, the ovule develops into a seed.

• **perennial** A plant that lives year after year.

• **petals** Arranged around the reproductive parts of a flower, usually brightly colored to attract pollinators.

• **photosynthesis** Green plants produce their own food. They do this by using energy from sunlight. The green substance in their leaves – chlorophyll – absorbs the sun's energy. Plants then take in water from the soil and carbon dioxide from the air and use the energy to convert them into a sugar for food.

• **pigment** Colors in leaves that show through in autumn when the normal green color from chlorophyll is masked.

• **pollinate** To transfer pollen from the anther (male part) to the stigma (female part) of a flower.

• **potting mix** A mixture of materials such as peat, pine bark, sawdust, and sand, ideal for growing plants in pots. It is available ready-made in bags from plant nurseries.

• **proboscis** A tube similar to a drinking straw beneath the head of an insect, used to suck liquids and nectar from flowers.

• **propagate** To grow a new plant either from a seed or by striking cuttings from an old plant.

• **ripe** When a fruit or vegetable has reached maturity and is ready to eat.

◆ **root** The underground part of a plant that anchors it in place and takes up water and food for the plant.

◆ **runner** A long stem that falls on the ground. Where it comes in contact with the soil, a new baby plant will grow.

◆ **sap** The fluid, made up of water and food, that circulates through a plant.

◆ **seed** Comes from the fruit of a plant. When planted, it will grow into a new plant.

◆ **seedbed** A garden bed, with well-dug and raked soil (even and crumbly), especially used for raising seeds.

◆ **seedling** A small plant about 2 inches (5 cm) high which has grown from a seed.

◆ **seed saving** Keeping any seeds from your flowers in the garden or from the fruit and vegetables you eat. These saved seeds can be used to grow new plants.

◆ **seed sowing** Placing seed either in soil in the garden or in potting mix in a pot and watering.

◆ **shoot** A shoot grows out of the seed and upward, forming the stem of a plant.

◆ **shoots** When a plant begins to grow.

◆ **soil** Composed of mineral matter (from broken-down rocks), dead and living plant and animal matter, and air and water.

◆ **shrub** A plant with a bushy habit.

◆ **sprout** When a seed begins to grow shoots and roots.

◆ **tamper** A flat piece of wood with a centered stick of wood to hold on to, used to press down the potting mix in a seed tray.

◆ **tendril** A threadlike leaf or stem that attaches to a support by twining around it.

◆ **topsoil** The upper part of the soil, between the leaf litter at the top and the layers below that are bedrock and weathering rock.

◆ **transplant** To move a plant from one place to another. You can start seeds off in a pot and then transplant them to the garden at seedling stage.

◆ **tree** A fairly long-lived plant that has a trunk and branches forming a canopy.

◆ **trowel** A small shovel.

◆ **tuber** A swollen stem, growing underground, such as a potato.

◆ **unripe** A fruit or vegetable that has not yet reached maturity and is not edible.

◆ **variegated** Patches of different colors on the leaves of a plant.

◆ **variety** A type of plant that differs slightly from the species.

◆ **well-ventilated** A position where plenty of air can flow in and around the plant.